SOMALIA
in Pictures

Janice Hamilton

TF
CB
Twenty-First Century Books

Contents

Lerner Publishing Group realizes that current information and statistics quickly become out of date. To extend the usefulness of the Visual Geography Series, we developed www.vgsbooks.com, a website offering links to up-to-date information, as well as in-depth material, on a wide variety of subjects. All of the websites listed on www.vgsbooks.com have been carefully selected by researchers at Lerner Publishing Group. However, Lerner Publishing Group is not responsible for the accuracy or suitability of the material on any website other than www.lernerbooks.com. It is recommended that students using the Internet be supervised by a parent or teacher. Links on www.vgsbooks.com will be regularly reviewed and updated as needed.

Twenty-First Century Books
A division of Lerner Publishing Group
241 First Avenue North
Minneapolis, MN 55401 U.S.A.

Website address: www.lernerbooks.co

web enhanced @ www.vgsbooks.com

CULTURAL LIFE 48

▶ Religion. The Somali Language. Poetry. Stories and Theater. Music. Clothing and Weaving. Food. Sports and Games. Holidays and Festivals.

THE ECONOMY 56

▶ Sources of Income. Livestock. Crop Production. Trade. Transportation. Energy. Media and Communications. Somaliland: A Struggling Economy. The Future.

FOR MORE INFORMATION

Library of Congress Cataloging-in-Publication Data

Hamilton, Janice.
    Somalia in pictures / by Janice Hamilton.
        p.   cm. – (Visual geography series)
    Includes bibliographical references and index.
    ISBN-13: 978-0-8225-6586-4 (lib. bdg. : alk. paper)
    ISBN-10: 0-8225-6586-2 (lib. bdg. : alk. paper)
    1. Somalia—Juvenile literature. 2. Somalia—Pictorial works—Juvenile literature. I. Title. II. Series:
Visual geography series (Minneapolis, Minn.)
DT401.5.H35 2007
967.73—dc22   2006016542

Manufactured in the United States of America
1 2 3 4 5 6 – BP – 12 11 10 09 08 07

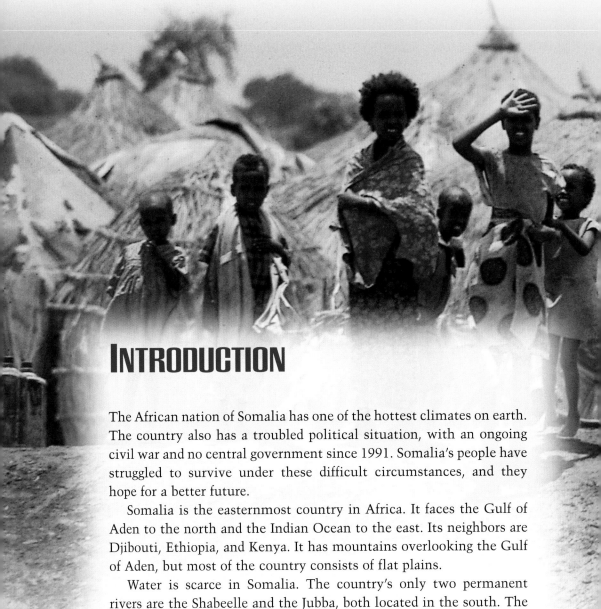

INTRODUCTION

The African nation of Somalia has one of the hottest climates on earth. The country also has a troubled political situation, with an ongoing civil war and no central government since 1991. Somalia's people have struggled to survive under these difficult circumstances, and they hope for a better future.

Somalia is the easternmost country in Africa. It faces the Gulf of Aden to the north and the Indian Ocean to the east. Its neighbors are Djibouti, Ethiopia, and Kenya. It has mountains overlooking the Gulf of Aden, but most of the country consists of flat plains.

Water is scarce in Somalia. The country's only two permanent rivers are the Shabeelle and the Jubba, both located in the south. The weather is usually dry, but sometimes heavy rains cause flooding.

Somalia's economy is based on livestock herding and agriculture. Herders raise camels, which can live for long periods without water, as well as hardy goats and sheep. Herders in the south also raise cattle. Many herders are nomadic, meaning they move about the countryside

with their animals, in search of grazing land and water. Herders cannot remain in one spot for long. If too many animals remain near one water source, they eat up all the nearby grass and shrubs.

Most people raise animals to sell for cash. Livestock also provides families with milk and meat. The region around and between the Shabeelle and Jubba rivers is a crop-growing area. Farmers there grow bananas, citrus fruits, vegetables, and grains.

Eighty-five percent of Somalis belong to the Somali ethnic group. Almost everyone in Somalia practices the Islamic religion. Each person is also a member of a clan, a large group of families that trace their common ancestry through many generations of fathers. Although most Somalis share the same culture, intense rivalries between clans have divided Somali society.

Humans have lived in the region that would become Somalia for thousands of years. Starting about 700 A.D., Arabs and Persians began to settle in Somalia. These newcomers introduced Islam to native Somalis.

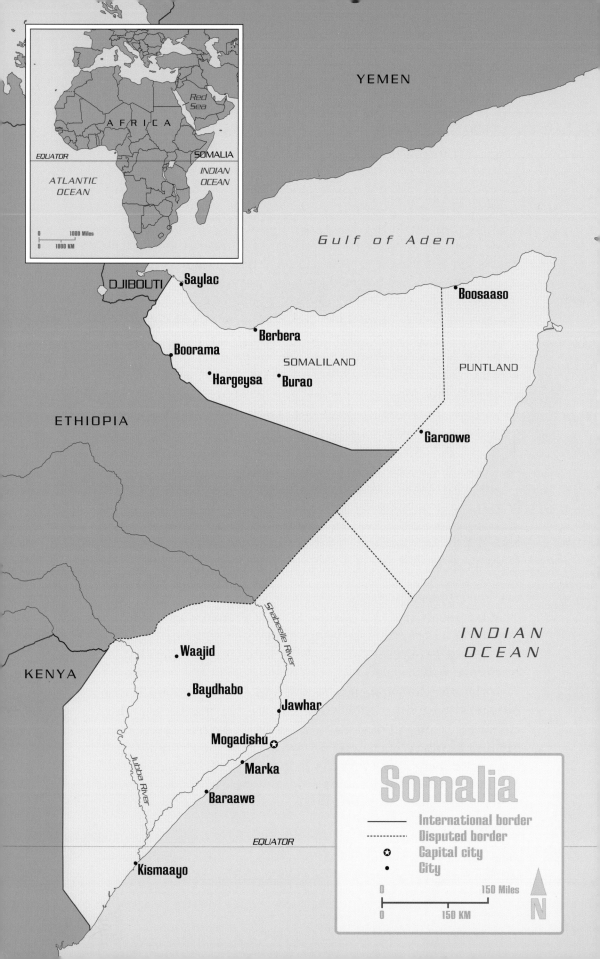

By the late 1800s, the British controlled northern Somalia (called British Somaliland), and the Italians controlled southern Somalia (Italian Somaliland). Somalia became independent in 1960. The city of Mogadishu was the nation's capital. But in 1969, military rebels broke up the National Assembly, the nation's lawmaking body, and canceled the constitution. General Mohamed Siad Barre ruled Somalia as a dictator—a leader with absolute power. Rebels forced him from office in 1991. The country then fell into chaos and conflict. A civil war developed. The United States and the United Nations (an international peacekeeping organization) sent soldiers to try to restore peace.

Even after the civil war died down, fighting broke out occasionally, especially in Mogadishu. In 2004 Somali politicians established the Transitional Federal Government (TFG), a temporary government. But Somalia was so dangerous that TFG leaders remained in nearby countries. The TFG did not truly run the country. Powerful criminals called warlords controlled most of southern and central Somalia, including cities and ports. Militias—armed soldiers hired by the warlords—protected the warlords' territories. In 2006 a militia fighting for an Islamic organization, the Islamic Courts Union, took control of Mogadishu and other parts of Somalia. The TFG then fought the Islamic Courts Union for control of Somalia.

In the northwest, a territory called the Republic of Somaliland has broken away from the rest of Somalia. Somaliland has an elected president and legislature. But other governments refuse to recognize Somaliland's independence. In the northeast, the region known as Puntland has also set up its own government. Somaliland and Puntland are not entirely peaceful, but they are much more stable than the rest of Somalia.

Many people who fled violent areas of Somalia have settled in Somaliland and Puntland. In addition, more than one million Somalis have left their homeland entirely. Many have settled in Great Britain, North America, or Australia.

With its harsh environment and political difficulties, Somalia is an extremely poor country. Diseases such as diarrhea, malaria, and tuberculosis are common. Many children die before age five. Few Somalis can read because schools were destroyed during the civil war. If and when a national government takes control over this shattered country, it will face many challenges.

THE LAND

Somalia, officially named the Somali Democratic Republic, is located in the Horn of Africa, a region that resembles a rhinoceros horn. With an area of approximately 246,201 square miles (637,657 square kilometers), Somalia is slightly smaller than the U.S. state of Texas.

Somalia is shaped like the number seven. Across the top, the Gulf of Aden (an arm of the Indian Ocean) separates Somalia from the Arabian Peninsula. The nation's long eastern coast faces the Indian Ocean. Somalia's coastline totals 1,880 miles (3,025 km) and is the longest in Africa. Somalia shares its southern border with Kenya. Ethiopia lies to the west, and Djibouti sits to the northwest.

Regions

In the north, the low-lying Guban Plain sits next to the Gulf of Aden. The sun scorches the Guban Plain, and plant life there is sparse.

South of the Guban are the Kar Kar Mountains. They extend from the Ethiopian border to northeastern Somalia. The mountains rise

more than 6,000 feet (1,828 meters) above sea level. Surud Ad, the country's highest mountain at 7,900 feet (2,408 m), is located here. This rugged region consists of cliffs, steep valleys, and few roads. Riverbeds are dry for much of the year.

South of the mountains is the Ogo Plateau, which sits about 3,940 feet (1,200 m) above sea level. In the southwest, the plateau descends to the Haud Plain. It is a reddish, sandy plain that provides good grazing land for livestock. Toward the east, the plateau slopes toward the Indian Ocean.

Central Somalia is known as the Mudug Plain. The broad Nugaaleed Valley cuts across the northern part of the plain. The rivers that carved the valley are dry for much of the year. The soil in this region has a lot of salt and is not good for farming.

The major features of southern Somalia are gently sloping coastal plains and the wide valleys of the Shabeelle and Jubba rivers. Fertile soil between the rivers, combined with more water, makes southern

Somalia the country's main agricultural area. The southern coastal region is known as the Benadir Coast.

▶ Rivers

Somalia has no lakes and only two large rivers. The Jubba River flows south from its source in southern Ethiopia. After crossing the Somali border, it continues about 545 miles (875 km) before emptying into the Indian Ocean north of the port city of Kismaayo. The Jubba is the only river in Somalia with a year-round water supply. Although the river is shallow, flat-bottomed boats can navigate its southern portions during the rainy months. A fertile farming region surrounds the Jubba.

The Shabeelle, Somalia's only other major river, also begins in the Ethiopian highlands. For most of its length of 1,130 miles (1,820 km), it flows southeastward. About 20 miles (32 km) from the Indian Ocean, the river turns to the southwest and continues parallel to the sea. During the rainy season, the waters of the Shabeelle join the Jubba north of Kismaayo. In dry seasons, the Shabeelle simply disappears into a marshy area and never reaches the sea.

A boy pushes a raft through his flooded village on the **Jubba River** in southern Somalia.

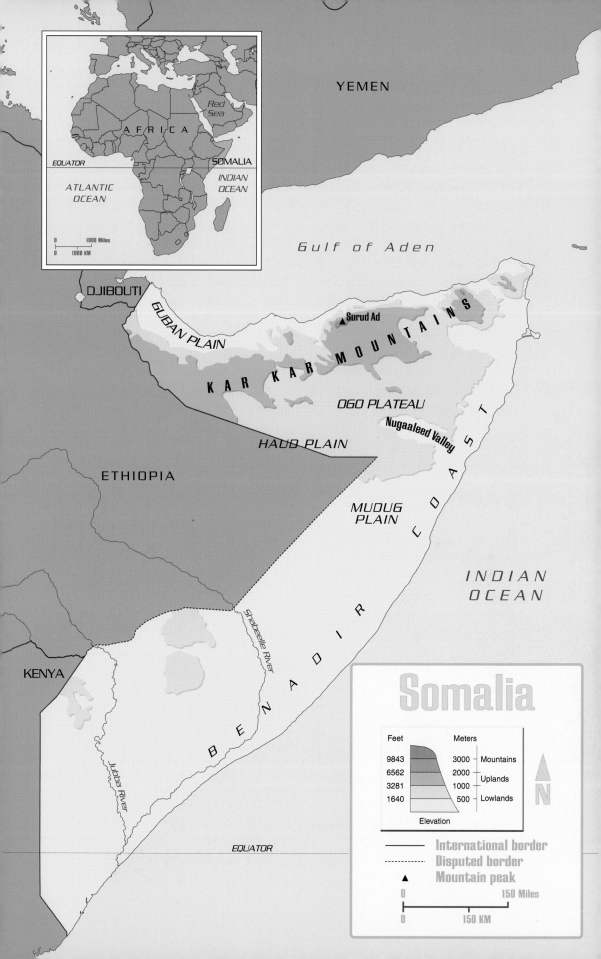

YEMEN

Gulf of Aden

DJIBOUTI

GUBAN PLAIN

▲ Surud Ad

K A R   K A R   M O U N T A I N S

OGO PLATEAU

Nugaaleed Valley

HAUD PLAIN

ETHIOPIA

MUDUG PLAIN

INDIAN OCEAN

B E N A D I R   C O A S T

Shabeelle River

KENYA

Jubba River

EQUATOR

Inset map
YEMEN
Red Sea
AFRICA
EQUATOR
SOMALIA
ATLANTIC OCEAN
INDIAN OCEAN

0   1000 Miles
0   1000 KM

Somalia

Feet	Meters	
9843	3000	Mountains
6562	2000	Uplands
3281	1000	
1640	500	Lowlands

Elevation

N

——— International border
- - - - Disputed border
▲ Mountain peak

0   150 Miles
0   150 KM

A CLIMATE OF EXTREMES

Droughts occur about every eight to ten years in Somalia. These extreme dry periods are especially serious when the long gu rains fail—and fail for several seasons in a row. Recent severe droughts occurred in 1975, 1992, and 2005.

During a drought, the soil becomes cracked and hard. Trees become bare and brittle, crops die, and any remaining grass is bleached by the sun. Vultures gorge themselves on the bodies of dead livestock. Cattle are generally the first to die. Goats and especially camels are able to survive longer without water. In a severe drought, even the camels die. People might die, too.

As the wet season approaches, clouds build up in the sky for days. Finally, the rain begins. Sometimes only light showers fall. Other times, the clouds bring heavy downpours with thunder and lightening. Roads turn to mud. Water roars through usually dry riverbeds, sometimes sweeping away small animals and children, or overflowing riverbanks. Within a few weeks, the grass is several feet tall. Wildflowers, butterflies, and insects are everywhere.

◉ Climate

The equator, an imaginary line separating the northern and southern parts of the earth, passes through the southern tip of Somalia. Places near the equator, including Somalia, have some of the hottest weather on earth. The city of Berbera, on the northern coast, is the hottest place in Somalia. The thermometer exceeds 100°F (38°C) there every afternoon from June to September. Along the Indian Ocean coast, a cold current of water cools the land somewhat. The average temperature in the coastal city of Mogadishu is 79°F (26°C) in January and 78° F (26°C) in July. In the mountains, temperatures are cooler.

Somalia has four seasons, two wet and two dry. The main rainy season, called the *gu*, lasts from April to June. It is followed by the *xagaa*, a dry season that continues through September. Even during the xagaa, some rain falls along the coast. A second wet season, the *dayr*, occurs from October to December. The main dry season, the *jilaal*, lasts from December through March.

The northeast, the nation's driest area, receives less than 4 inches (10 centimeters) of rain a year. Central Somalia averages between 8 and 12 inches (20 to 30 cm) of rain a year. The southwest and the northwest receive an average 20 to 24 inches (50 to 60 cm) a year. Every eight or ten years, severe drought hits Somalia. Rivers dry up, and crops and livestock die.

⊘ Flora and Fauna

Somalia is rich in wildlife. It has about two hundred bird and animal species found nowhere else on earth. It is home to approximately five thousand different species of plants. Plant and animal species found here have adapted to survive in the dry environment.

Grasses and shrubs are the most common plants in Somalia. They grow in the nation's many dry areas. Evergreens and aloe plants also live in dry areas. Flat-topped acacia trees and thorny commiphora trees (which produce a fragrant substance called myrrh) grow in places with more rainfall. In mountainous areas, plants include evergreen bushes and juniper trees. Some juniper trees stand more than 65 feet (20 m) high. Somalia's long coastline features sea grasses and mangrove forests.

Large mammals in Somalia include the dibitag, a slender antelope with a long neck. The Speke's gazelle is another antelope native to Somalia. It makes a sneezelike alarm noise when it feels threatened. Soemmerring's gazelles and

THE AFRICAN WILD ASS

The African wild ass *(left)*, the wild ancestor of the donkey, once lived across northern Africa, from Morocco to Somalia. The animal has a gray back, white belly, and striped legs. It is related to the zebra. African wild asses can live on very little water. They usually rest under shady bushes in the daytime and become more active in the evening and in cool weather.

In the early 1900s, about ten thousand African wild asses lived in the stony, arid hills of Somalia. But people hunted and killed the asses for food. The asses also had to compete for scarce water with herd animals. The asses began to die out. Eventually, the African wild ass became one of the world's rarest animals. In 2002 one scientist estimated Somalia's wild ass population at just ten.

British botanist Jan Gillett stands next to a **giant termite tower.** For links to more information on termite towers, go to www.vgsbooks.com.

rare beira antelopes live in the mountains. Leopards, cheetahs, and hyenas are the main predators (hunting species) in Somalia. Small mammals include the walo, a type of gerbil found only in Somalia. Small rodents called naked mole rats (also called sand puppies) live in underground colonies.

As for birds, several species of larks and hornbills are common. The Somali pigeon, the Somali thrush, and the Warsangli linnet make their homes in the mountains. Lots of insects live in Somalia. In digging their nests, termites and ants create cone-shaped mounds that sometimes reach more than 12 feet (3 m) high. Snakes and lizards are also common in Somalia.

A variety of fish, shellfish, and wading birds live along the coast. A long coral reef (an underwater ridge made from the skeletons of billions of small sea animals) sits about one-half mile (0.8 km) off Somalia's southern coast. Other coral reefs run along the Gulf of Aden coast. The reefs are home to fish and other sea animals.

Natural Resources

Somalia's main economic resource is grazing land. People use this land to raise sheep, goats, and camels. They also raise cattle in the south. Most herders raise livestock to sell for cash. They also keep some animals for milk and meat.

Somalia has fertile farmland between the Shebeelle and Jubba rivers, an area known as the riverine region. Farmers there grow bananas, citrus fruits, vegetables, cotton, and grains. But pumps and ditches that once carried extra water from the rivers to the fields were damaged during the civil war. As a result, Somalia's farming output has declined since the war.

Somalia has extensive marine (ocean) resources. Large fish, including yellowfin tuna and bonito, swim offshore. Lobsters, groupers, snappers, and several types of sharks live near coral reefs. In coastal villages, fishers catch sea animals from small boats close to shore. They and their families eat their catches rather than sell them.

Somalia has deposits of uranium, iron ore, tin, gypsum, bauxite, copper, and salt. But because of warfare, little mining takes place. Somalia also has untapped stores of natural gas. Some people suspect the nation has oil reserves. Oil companies are unable to explore for oil because the country is too dangerous.

Somalia sorely lacks the most basic natural resource, water. Water is so precious that people often fight over it. Some communities have shared wells. Some landowners have private wells and charge people to use them. Systems that once supplied water in cities such as Mogadishu were destroyed during the civil war. There is no government to build new wells, pipes, and pumps or to look for new underground water sources.

◉ Environmental Concerns

Somalia has many environmental problems. Some of them stem from natural causes. Others are linked to war, politics, and poverty.

Livestock herding, the most common job in Somalia, is hard on the land. Thousands of goats, sheep, and other livestock eat wild grasses and shrubs. But if the animals stay too long in one place, the grasses and shrubs disappear, especially during the dry seasons. Herders have to wait for rain and for the plants to grow back.

TSUNAMI

On December 26, 2004, an underwater earthquake off the coast of Indonesia created a tsunami, or massive wave. The wave slammed into lands around the Indian Ocean, destroying homes and killing more than 130,000 people. It left many thousands homeless.

The tsunami reached as far as Somalia, more than 4,000 miles (6,436 km) from Indonesia. The huge wave roared inland along a 400-mile (650-km) stretch of the Indian Ocean coast. The wave killed an estimated 150 Somalis and destroyed the homes and livelihoods of about eighteen thousand families. It ripped fishing gear apart and tossed small boats inland. Salty ocean water contaminated ponds and wells. The wave also spread human waste and garbage, as well as hazardous industrial wastes that had been stored on beaches.

A Somali woman buys charcoal in Mogadishu.

THE CHARCOAL TRADE

Somalis have long used charcoal in their homes for cooking. Charcoal is also one of the country's biggest exports. To prepare charcoal, people chop down trees, stack the wood tightly, cover it with earth to limit the amount of available oxygen, and set it on fire. Without much oxygen, the wood does not burn completely. The partially burned pieces of wood are charcoal. In the past, woodcutters used axes to cut down trees. In modern times, woodcutters use chainsaws, and warlords largely control the business.

More than 80 percent of Somalis use wood for cooking. In rural areas, people cut down trees for firewood. In cities, they cook with charcoal, which is made from partially burned wood. Merchants also sell charcoal to other countries. People also cut trees for building homes and other structures. As a result, acacia, mangrove, and other trees are rapidly disappearing. Trees provide shade and shelter for wildlife, and their roots hold the soil in place. Cutting down trees in great numbers damages the soil and hurts plants and animals.

At one time, the beisa oryx, a large antelope with long horns, was found throughout Somalia. But poaching (illegal hunting) has wiped out the animals. As recently as 1980, an estimated forty thousand elephants lived in Somalia. But poachers have shot most of the elephants for their valuable ivory tusks. Similarly, lions were once common predators on the plains. But only an estimated 500 to 750 remain. In the 1970s and 1980s, the Somali government passed laws to protect wildlife from illegal hunting and other dangers. But these laws exist on paper only. No one actually looks after wildlife or polices illegal hunting.

Somalia has few laws to prevent pollution. In fact, some corrupt Somali politicians and businesspeople allow foreign companies to dump containers of toxic chemicals and industrial wastes on Somali beaches. Oil pollution is another threat. Numerous oil tankers sail off the Somali coast on their way to and from the Persian Gulf. A major oil spill could destroy Somalia's beaches. Meanwhile, workers at Somali ports do not have the knowledge or equipment to clean up even small oil spills.

Since the Somali government fell in 1991, foreign fishing vessels have been fishing illegally in Somali waters. Usually operating in the dark, they use destructive fishing techniques. For example, some fishers blast coral reefs with dynamite, killing all the animals there.

Cities

MOGADISHU, with an estimated population of 1.18 million, is the country's largest city. It is the official capital of Somalia. However, as of mid-2006, the president and some other members of the transitional government were unable to go to Mogadishu because it was too dangerous.

Founded in the 900s, Mogadishu was one of the earliest Arab settlements on the coast of East Africa. It was a large port city by the 1300s, but trade declined in the 1500s. The sultan, or king, of Zanzibar (a territory south of Somalia) took control of the city in 1871. Later, Mogadishu was the capital of Italian Somaliland and then of independent Somalia. It was a beautiful city with a mixture of Somali, Arab, and Italian architecture, gleaming white buildings, and green trees.

Visit www.vgsbooks.com for links to websites with additional information about Mogadishu and other Somali cities. See pictures of what life in Mogadishu is like.

However, years of civil war reduced the city to ruins. The city's factories closed, and thieves took the goods and equipment. Thieves even stole and resold the city's telephone wires. Armed militias working for powerful warlords patrolled the city in "technicals," or trucks outfitted with heavy weapons. Fighting broke out frequently. Mogadishu has become one of the most dangerous cities in the world, and few foreigners visit it.

HARGEYSA, on the plateau near the Ethiopian border, was for a time the capital of British Somaliland. Somali government forces almost destroyed the city in 1988, while they were fighting rebel forces. When Somaliland declared independence in 1991, Hargeysa became the new country's capital. Residents have built new hotels, hospitals, and other facilities. They are especially proud of the city's traffic lights. The city has grown rapidly in recent years, as residents who left during the war have returned home. The current population is between 300,000 and 400,000.

KISMAAYO is a seaport city in southern Somalia. No one has counted its people since 1981, when the population was 70,000. The city is located on the Indian Ocean near the mouth of the Jubba River. The sultan of Zanzibar founded Kismaayo in 1871. During the early twentieth century, the city was an important port in Italian Somaliland. It is still a port city, primarily shipping cattle and bananas to other nations.

Left: In the 1920s, **Mogadishu** offered an impressive mix of architecture and culture. Structures included a grand arch *(far left)*, a large Catholic church *(center)* and an Islamic house of worship *(right)*. *Below:* In recent years, the city has been **devastated by civil war** and many of the buildings have crumbled.

BERBERA, located on the Gulf of Aden, is Somaliland's main port. Its population totaled 65,000 in 1981, the last time a count was taken. The town dates to at least the 1200s. Several foreign powers, including the Portuguese in 1518 and the British in 1884, have attacked and conquered the city over the centuries. Berbera served as the capital of British Somaliland until 1941, when the capital moved to Hargeysa. In modern times, merchants here export (sell to other countries) sheep, animal skins and hides, and a fragrant substance called frankincense.

Other urban centers in Somalia include Marka on the Indian Ocean coast and Baydhabo in the interior. In Puntland, the town of Boosaaso, on the Gulf of Aden, is the main business center, and Garoowe is the government center. Other Somaliland cities include Burao and Boorama.

HISTORY AND GOVERNMENT

People have lived in Somalia for thousands of years. But there are few written accounts of Somalia's early history. Thousands of years ago, people in Somalia passed on knowledge only orally. That is, each generation of Somalis told stories or poems about historic events to the next generation. Ancient Somalis also communicated with images. Archaeologists have found ancient cave paintings near Hargeysa. The paintings include pictures of donkeys, goats, a cow, and a person praying to the cow.

About 2200 B.C., travelers from ancient Egypt first visited a place they called the Land of Punt. Historians aren't sure where Punt was, but it likely included Somalia and southwestern Arabia. Egyptian merchants visited Punt to buy frankincense and myrrh. The ancient Greeks began to trade with Punt in the late fourth century B.C.

Ancient Somalia was home to several ethnic groups, including the Somali, Afar, Oromo, Bantu, and Wa-Ribi peoples. Depending on where they lived, people made a living by herding livestock, farming, hunting, and fishing.

In about A.D. 700, settlers from Arabia and Persia (modern-day Iran) began to establish settlements along the Somali coast. The most important of these towns was Saylac, located in the northwestern corner of modern Somaliland. Traders from Abyssinia (modern-day Ethiopia) used Saylac's harbor to ship goods to Arabia and Asia. The traders sold animal hides, ostrich feathers, frankincense, slaves, and ivory to foreign merchants. They bought cloth, dates, pottery, weapons, and iron shipped in from Arabia and Asia.

Arabs and Persians created the city of Mogadishu around 900. In the early 1000s, an Arab sheik (chief) named Daarood Jabarti settled in northeastern Somalia and married Doombira Dir, the daughter of the local chief. His descendents formed the powerful Darod clan. About two hundred years later, another Arab founded the Isaaq clan. Eventually, the Somalis created a myth about their Arab origins. They said that all Somalis were descended from one Arab ancestor. His name was Samaale or Somaal.

Arab culture had a big impact on Somalia. Arab merchants and sailors introduced the religion of Islam, which the prophet Muhammad had founded on the Arabian Peninsula in the 600s. Between 1000 and 1300, large numbers of Somalis became Muslims (followers of Islam). The Arabs also introduced a system of tracking generations through the father.

People on the Move

After 1200, many Somalis began to move from the north to the south. Historians are not sure why. Perhaps people were fleeing a serious drought in the north. Or perhaps the growing population needed room to expand. As they migrated, they pushed other people off the land. The Somalis forced Oromo herders to leave the interior, and they displaced Bantu farmers from the fertile south. During this period, Mogadishu was an important trading city, famous for its woven cotton cloth.

While many people in the Horn of Africa were Muslims, their neighbors in Ethiopia were Christians. At first, the two groups got along well. But in the early 1400s, a long period of conflict began. Saad ad-Din was the sultan of the Islamic state of Ifat, centered at Saylac. He called for a war against "Christian infidels." (*Infidel* is an insulting name for someone who does not believe in a particular religion, in this case Islam.) His troops invaded Ethiopia, burned Christian churches, and forced captives to convert to Islam.

Then the tide turned. The Ethiopians chased the sultan to an island near Saylac and killed him in 1415. After this victory, the Ethiopian king commanded musicians to write a hymn thanking God for this success against the Muslims. The hymn contained the word *Somali*—probably the first time it was written anywhere.

In 1499 a Portuguese expedition sailed up the east coast of Africa. The Portuguese were looking for gold, ivory, slaves, and other resources. Portuguese troops attacked Mogadishu but failed to capture it. They continued attacks along the Somali coast over the next twenty years but never gained permanent control there.

Ifat, which by then was called Adal, became a powerful state again in the early 1500s. Saylac became a prosperous port with schools and beautiful mosques (Islamic houses of worship). Muslim forces grew strong enough to take on the Ethiopians again. Their religious and military leader, Ahmad Guray, attracted many followers. He declared a jihad, or holy war, against the Ethiopians.

Somali nomads, especially members of the Darod clan, made up a large part of Ahmad Guray's army. They invaded Ethiopia, burning the countryside and killing many citizens. By 1535 Muslim forces controlled most of central Ethiopia and had converted many

Portuguese explorers sailed the coast of Africa looking for wealth and an easy way to India. They often used violence to try to gain control of the coast.

Ethiopians to Islam. But eventually, a new Ethiopian ruler came to the throne, rearmed the troops, and enlisted the help of the Portuguese to fight the Somalis.

By then the Portuguese controlled key outposts along the east coast of Africa, the Red Sea, the Persian Gulf, and the ocean route between Europe and India. Portuguese troops helped the Ethiopians defeat the Muslim invaders. Ahmad Guray died in battle in 1543.

Foreign Powers

Portugal was not the only foreign nation interested in the riches of Africa. Other European nations explored and set up colonies in Africa, as well as in the Middle East and Asia. In 1839 the British established a coaling station (to supply coal to ships on their way to the British colony in India) at Aden in Yemen, across the Gulf of Aden from Somalia. The British in Yemen relied on Somalia as a source of meat. Herders brought their sheep to Saylac and Berbera and shipped them across the gulf to the British.

Europeans also explored Somalia itself. French explorer Charles Guillain traveled along the southern coast in 1847. He found Mogadishu in ruins following a famine and an outbreak of plague. In 1854 British explorer Sir Richard Burton visited Saylac, then traveled

EXPEDITION TO HARER

In the mid-1800s, Africa fascinated many Europeans. Much of East Africa was unexplored. No European or Christian had ever been inside the walled city of Harer (in modern-day Ethiopia). Local legend warned that Harer's ruler would lose his independence once a Christian entered the city.

A former British military officer, explorer Richard Burton (*right*), wanted to visit Harer and then undertake a major expedition from Berbera to Zanzibar. Burton spoke several languages, including Arabic. He spent three months in Saylac, organizing a train of servants, camels, mules, and supplies for the trip to Harer.

In *First Footsteps in East Africa*, published in 1859, Burton described his trip across the hot plains and into the mountains. En route, he encountered many local peoples—some friendly, others not—and wild animals including lions, elephants, and hyenas. He traveled disguised as a Turkish merchant but changed into European clothes before entering Harer. He was relieved when the city's ruler greeted him with a smile.

inland to Harer in Ethiopia. A year later, Burton was camped at Berbera, planning an expedition to the interior. Several hundred Somali fighters, armed with spears, attacked his party. The Somalis killed or badly wounded several officers and speared Burton in the mouth. He survived and escaped to Aden. The British Royal Geographical Society, which had sponsored the expedition, blamed Burton for the attack. He never returned to Somalia.

The French established ports in modern-day Djibouti around 1862. In 1869 the Suez Canal, a human-made waterway linking the Mediterranean and Red seas, opened for business. The canal greatly shortened the sea voyage between Europe and Asia. It also

increased the strategic importance of East Africa and the Middle East. The British, French, Italians, Egyptians, and Ethiopians all competed for control of Somalia and surrounding territories.

Also in 1869, the Italians purchased a port in Eritrea, north of Somalia. Egypt took over territory and ports along the Gulf of Aden coast. After the Egyptians left to deal with a revolt elsewhere, the British took control of the former Egyptian ports. The British also signed treaties with the main Somali clans. The British guaranteed the clans their independence, while Britain maintained law and order and controlled trade in Somalia.

Many Somalis were hostile to foreigners, but they were unable to mount a strong resistance. Their only weapons were spears and daggers, because the Europeans refused to sell guns to Muslims. Also, many clans disliked one another, so the Somalis were unable to form a united front.

Meanwhile, a French-British rivalry heated up. The French expanded their territory in Djibouti and established a coaling station to supply ships en route to their colonies in Southeast Asia. The British and the French came close to war to protect their interests in the region. But in 1888, they agreed on the boundaries of their territories.

In 1889 Italy and Ethiopia signed a treaty. The Italians gave the Ethiopians money and rifles. The Ethiopians used these arms to attack Somali herders in the countryside around Harer. Although the British had agreed to protect the Somalis, they did not do so.

In the same year, Italy acquired land in Somalia. It rented several ports along the southern Benadir Coast and took control of Mogadishu. The local Somali clans signed treaties, placing themselves under the protection of the Italians. Meanwhile, Somali areas south of the Jubba River remained in British hands.

Many Somalis resented the Europeans. In Italian-held areas, the Italians treated Somalis as conquered people rather than equals. Several times, Somali fighters attacked and killed small parties of Italians. The Italian administration cracked down to restore order. At the same time, Somalis south of the Jubba River rebelled against the British.

In the early 1890s, the British and the Italians signed agreements concerning their territories in Somalia. The agreements said that Britain would control the north coast and the interior Haud Plain, while Italy would control the northeast, the southern coast, and the interior.

Meanwhile, relations between the Ethiopians and the Italians deteriorated. The Ethiopians did not want the Italians to control them. They took up arms to defend their homeland. The conflict came to a head in 1896 at Adowa, in the mountains of Ethiopia. There, well-armed Ethiopian forces achieved a resounding victory over the Italians.

Within sight of Ethiopia's mountains, Ethiopian troops confronted Italian forces at the **Battle of Adowa in 1896.**

After the Battle of Adowa, the Italians recognized Ethiopian independence. Meanwhile, in 1897 the French began to build a railway from central Ethiopia to the port of Djibouti, in what was then called French Somaliland.

During this period, small groups of Ethiopian fighters attacked Somali nomad camps and villages as far south as the Jubba River. The Somalis still did not have guns, so they were unable to fight back. The British were fed up. They did not want to invest much effort in protecting the Somali clans, and they abandoned their agreement to protect a large section of the Haud Plain. As a result, many ethnic Somalis who lived in the Haud region ended up under Ethiopian rule without being consulted or even informed.

By the end of the nineteenth century, the Somali people were split between British Somaliland, Italian Somaliland, and French Somaliland, as well as Ethiopia. But the boundaries between these territories were vague, and this confusion resulted in conflict.

The Dervish Resistance

The end of the nineteenth century also saw a strong Somali resistance movement in the north. Mahammad Abdille Hasan led the movement. His skills as a poet and speaker—and as a peacemaker between warring clans—gained him many followers. He believed the British, who were Christians and therefore infidels in his eyes, were destroying the Muslim religion. The British dismissed him as a religious fanatic and called him the Mad Mullah (a mullah is an Islamic religious leader). By 1899, five thousand Dervishes, as his followers were known, were ready to attack the foreigners.

In 1900 and 1904, the British launched four major military expeditions against the Dervishes. Despite several Dervish victories, Hasan's followers lost strength and determination. They withdrew into Italian territory, where they established a small religious state. While the Dervishes reorganized, the British moved their forces to the coast.

The British hoped the Somalis would find a leader to counter the Dervishes, but that did not happen. By this time, the Somalis had found merchants who would sell them guns. The clans began to settle old scores and rivalries. Soon there was chaos in the interior. Warfare disrupted food production. People began to starve—some were so hungry they ate rats. An estimated one-third of the population in the north had died by the end of 1912. The British failed to help the Somalis during this crisis, and this neglect gained the Dervishes new followers.

The British created a force of police officers, who traveled by camel to restore order. Commanded by Richard Corfield, the Camel Constabulary was quite successful. But when Corfield disobeyed orders and chased a large group of Dervish raiders, many men on both sides died, including Corfield. One of Hasan's most famous poems celebrated the British officer's death.

World War I broke out in Europe in 1914, and British leaders were too busy with the war to worry much about the Dervishes. In 1915, however, British forces captured a large Dervish fort and blockaded the coast to cut off the Dervish arms supply. After the world war ended in 1918, the British attacked the main Dervish stronghold, but Hasan escaped. The Dervish movement finally collapsed when Hasan died of influenza in 1920.

British and Italians

The 1920s saw differences begin to emerge between British Somaliland and Italian Somaliland. While the British invested little in their Somali territory, the Italians had big plans for their colony. The Italian government wanted settlers to move to the colony. It wanted to control the interior, encourage trade with Ethiopia, and develop the region as a source of agricultural products.

The Italians studied the Somali soil and climate, drilled wells, and built irrigation ditches. They planted bananas, cotton, citrus fruits, and sugarcane on land taken from local residents. They opened hospitals,

Catholic elementary schools, and a government-run school to teach Somalis the Italian language. The Italians also built a cathedral (a large Catholic church) in Mogadishu. However, the colony was far from a success. It attracted few settlers and cost the Italian government far more money than it generated.

The British did far less with British Somaliland. They drilled some wells, opened schools for Somali children, and maintained law and order. But they did not invest in business and farming like the Italians did. Most Somalis viewed the British with hostility. They refused to send their children to the schools the British built for them.

By the mid-1930s, Italy was aggressively taking over territory in the Horn of Africa. In 1936 the Italian army overran Ethiopia entirely. World War II broke out in Europe 1939. The British and the Italians became enemies during the war. The Italians captured British Somaliland, but then the British retook the territory. They used it as a base to conquer the whole region and free Ethiopia from the Italians.

Meanwhile, some Somalis grew interested in national politics. They organized clubs to discuss their ideas. One such organization, the Somali Youth Club (SYC), formed in Mogadishu in 1943. It had members from all clans, and its members backed Somali nationalism. That is, they believed the Somali people should create a country of their own. They also wanted to end the old rivalries between the clans.

Preparing for Independence

After World War II ended in 1945, people in both Europe and Somalia discussed how to administer Somalia. The Italian government wanted its Somali territory returned. Some southern clans supported the Italians, but others bitterly opposed the idea. In 1949 the newly formed United Nations declared that Italy would control southern Somalia for ten years, after which it would become independent. In the north, British Somaliland was reestablished. The British ran the territory with the idea that it, too, would eventually be independent, but they set no timetable.

By this time, the SYC, with an estimated twenty-five thousand members, had changed its name to the Somali Youth League (SYL). Its aims included uniting all Somalis, giving children a modern education, and promoting the use of the Somali language and the Osmaniya script, a unique Somali alphabet. Other organizations with similar goals sprang up.

In preparation for independence, thousands of children and adults in southern Somalia enrolled in elementary schools. Adults took courses in government and leadership. The Italian administration built roads. Agricultural production increased.

In 1956 Somalis in the south voted for a seventy-seat legislative assembly. The SYL won the most votes in the election, and SYL leader Abdillahi Isa became Somalia's first prime minister. When the legislature expanded to ninety seats, the SYL again dominated it.

In the north, the British administration created a legislative council in 1957. At first, the British governor selected the council members. Later, in 1959, Somalis themselves were allowed to vote for some of the council members.

The Somali Republic

In 1960 political leaders agreed that Somalia would become a unified nation. It would be a democratic republic, with an elected president and a legislative assembly. The republic officially formed on July 1, 1960. Politicians from the north and south immediately met in Mogadishu and created the National Assembly. Somalis were optimistic about their country's future.

Problems soon appeared, however, especially between north and south. The economy was stronger in the south than in the north. Hargeysa's economy shrank, while Mogadishu became the busy national capital. There were no telephone links between these two cities.

By 1961 many northerners felt they were not benefiting from the new political arrangement. Many either refused to vote on the republic's new constitution, or they voted against it. In the south, an overwhelming majority of people approved the constitution.

Mohamed Ibrahim Egal *(left)* was the prime minister of Somalia in 1960 and from 1967 to 1969. Here he meets with the leaders of Kenya and Zambia to discuss the Kenya-Somalia border.

The Somali government saw clan loyalties as barriers to national unity. It encouraged people to put aside clan ties. But clans were not the only element that divided Somali society. There were misunderstandings between nomads, farmers, and people who made their living in towns. There was also a wide gap between the many poor Somalis and the few educated, wealthy Somalis. Language was another barrier. Everyone spoke Somali, but Italian was the language of government and business in the south, while people used English for government and business in the north.

Foreign governments stepped in to help the struggling young nation. They lent the Somali government money for economic development. The Soviet Union provided training and equipment to the armed forces, while the United States and Italy trained the police.

In the 1969 national election, the SYL won a large majority in the legislature, although internal rivalries caused deep divisions within the party. Meanwhile, disappointed citizens felt that National Assembly members ignored voters. Foreign aid money was flowing into the country, but much of it ended up in the pockets of corrupt politicians. After just nine years, the Somali experiment with democracy had soured.

Scientific Socialism

In October 1969, army officers, unhappy with the political situation, overthrew the elected Somali government. They shot and killed the president, occupied key points in Mogadishu, and jailed leading politicians. They abolished the Supreme Court, the National Assembly, and the constitution. They established a new ruling body called the Supreme Revolutionary Council (SRC) and renamed the country the Somali Democratic Republic. General Mohamed Siad Barre became president of the SRC.

Mohamed Siad Barre took over Somalia by force in 1969.

At first, the idealistic army officers planned to make positive changes in Somalia. They hoped to end rivalries between the clans. They wanted Somalis to fight poverty, disease, and ignorance rather than each other. They planned to replace inefficient and corrupt government employees with skilled administrators. They also wanted to teach people to read and write Somali and to publish laws, newspapers, and other documents in that language instead of English and Italian.

On the first anniversary of the takeover, General Siad Barre announced that Somalia would follow a policy he called Scientific Socialism. Socialism is an economic and political system in which the state owns and runs large parts of the economy, such as farms and factories. At the time, the Soviet Union and China were the world's most powerful and influential socialist countries.

Under Scientific Socialism, the Somali economy featured a mixture of private and state-owned businesses. The government owned the country's few large industries, including a Soviet-built meat-canning factory and a Chinese-built match factory. As part of the state-run economy, the government resettled 140,000 nomads into farming and coastal communities. The nomads had to give up herding animals and learn new job skills.

But corruption did not disappear, and the president became a powerful dictator in the 1970s. He did not allow people to express opposition to the government. He gave the most important jobs to his relatives. Many educated professionals disapproved of the government's policies and left the country during the 1970s.

In the early 1980s, opponents of the Somali government—both Somalis and Ethiopians—began to launch attacks into Somalia from across the Ethiopian border. As resistance to his government continued,

SOCIALISM IN SOMALIA

To promote Scientific Socialism, the Somali government borrowed many ideas from the socialist nations of the Soviet Union and China. Somalis greeted each other as *comrade*—a term used in the Soviet Union—rather than the traditional *cousin*. General Siad Barre's favorite sayings, such as "less talk and more work," were published in a little blue-and-white book (the colors of the Somali flag)—similar to the "Little Red Book" containing the sayings of Chinese leader Mao Tsetung. People called Siad Barre by titles such as Father of the State and Victorious Leader. The government set up training centers across the country, including at livestock watering places, to teach people the goals and methods of Scientific Socialism.

Siad Barre had many of his opponents tortured and killed. In 1986 his soldiers destroyed water supplies in regions that were home to enemy clans. As a result, thousands of people died of thirst.

Meanwhile, a group of Isaaq clan members living in England had formed the Somali National Movement (SNM) to oppose Siad Barre. The SNM organized clan members still living in Somalia. In 1988 SNM forces attacked government troops in the north, capturing Burao and part of Hargeysa. In response, Siad Barre's army bombed the two cities. The SNM withdrew, but the fighting resulted in the deaths of an estimated sixty thousand people and the destruction of wells and livestock grazing areas. More than three hundred thousand Somalis fled to Ethiopia for safety.

In 1989 Siad Barre's forces attacked the Hawiye clan in Mogadishu, killing many citizens and antigovernment demonstrators. The United States, which had for a time supported Siad Barre's government, revised its policy and cut back funding. In time, Siad Barre's opponents gained the upper hand in the fighting. The dictator's opponents scornfully called him the Mayor of Mogadishu, because by 1990 he controlled little more than the city. In January 1991, opposing clans finally forced Siad Barre from power.

Civil War

With Siad Barre gone, Somalia had no government, police force, or army. Warlords, mostly former army officers, formed private armies made up of fellow clan members. Civil war ensued. In the north, a few

Men in the militia loyal to warlord Mohammed Adid sit outside of Kismaayo in 1992.

months after Siad Barre was forced from office, the SNM announced that the former British territory was becoming the independent Republic of Somaliland.

In the south, warlords and their militias killed, beat, and raped members of minority ethnic groups and weaker clans. Mogadishu split into two armed zones controlled by rival warlords. An estimated fourteen thousand city residents died from violence or disease in 1991, the first year of the conflict.

The fighting disrupted food production, and famine spread throughout the south. Baydhabo was called the City of Death because so many people died there. Foreign groups sent emergency food supplies by airplane. But armed bandits stole most of the food before aid workers could distribute it.

People around the world wanted to help stop the famine. With the approval of the United Nations, the United States launched Operation Restore Hope in late 1992. U.S. Marines landed on the beaches of Mogadishu and took control of the city's port and airport. Troops from twenty-one other countries worked with the United States to protect the delivery of food and to try to restore peace. In 1993 the United Nations took over the operation, although U.S. troops remained.

In October 1993, U.S. Marines launched a helicopter attack on a house in Mogadishu, which they believed held a wanted warlord. A fierce gunfight broke out in the city streets. Two U.S. helicopters crashed, and eighteen U.S. troops and several hundred Somalis were killed. Angry with Americans interfering in Somali affairs, Somalis dragged the bodies of several dead U.S. marines through the streets. The United States pulled its troops out of Somalia. The last United Nations troops left Somalia in February 1995.

Trying to Establish a Government

After international troops left, much of the world seemed to wash its hands of Somalia. But neighboring nations wanted peace restored. Ethiopia, Djibouti, Kenya, and Yemen tried to help Somalis work out a solution.

Throughout the 1990s, neighboring countries hosted a series of peace conferences, and experts suggested ways to rebuild Somalia. Meanwhile, there was no longer full-scale civil war, but neither was there peace. Hostilities continued to flare up occasionally. Many people died when they accidentally stepped on hidden landmines left by enemy militias.

Various clans made alliances with each other. Power shifted as these groups fought to control valuable farmland and water sources. Warlords gained control over facilities such as ports, airports, and roads and forced people to pay to use them. Business leaders formed their own militias to protect their businesses.

Despite the conflict, people adapted, and daily life continued. Livestock herders cared for their animals. Market stalls, selling everything from tea to clothing, were open for business. There were no banks, but money changers acted as informal bankers. They changed money from other countries into Somali shillings.

There was no national court system, but most local courts still functioned. In some communities, clan elders (respected adult men) used traditional laws to resolve disputes. Other communities had sharia courts. These were courts that made rulings based on Islamic laws. In 1998 the northeastern region of Puntland broke with Somalia, declaring itself a self-governing territory.

In 2000 a meeting in Djibouti resulted in the establishment of a government called the Transitional National Government (TNG). It was a temporary government, meant to serve for three years. After that, Somalia was supposed to create a new constitution and hold elections.

On September 11, 2001, terrorists with links to al-Qaeda, an Islamist terrorist group, attacked the World Trade Center and other targets in the United States. Because Somalia is an Islamic country, the United States suspected that Islamist terrorists were hiding out in Somalia (Islamists are Muslims who want to establish Islamic societies governed by Islamic law). As the United States ramped up its "war on terror," it kept a close lookout for terrorist activities in Somalia.

In 2004, after more than two years of negotiations in Nairobi, Kenya, Somali politicians formed another temporary government, called the Transitional Federal Government (TFG). The government consisted of a 275-member legislature called the Transitional Federal Assembly. Each of the nation's four largest clans was assigned sixty-one seats in the assembly. The remaining thirty-one seats were divided between minority clans. Abdullahi Yusuf Ahmed, a warlord and the president of Puntland, became president of Somalia. But government leaders remained outside Somali borders because the country they were supposed to rule was so dangerous.

LOYALTY IN SOMALIA

A well-known Somali saying shows how Somalis stick together with family members. The saying goes: My full brother and I against my father, my father's household against my uncle's household, our two households against the rest of the immediate family, the immediate family against the distant members of my clan, my clan against other clans, and my nation and I against the world.

President Abdullahi Yusuf Ahmed speaks after winning the presidency in October 2004.

Meanwhile, Somaliland had created its own constitution. In 2005 its citizens held an election to select an eighty-two member House of Representatives. However, nations around the world wanted Somalia to remain united. They refused to recognize Somaliland as an independent country. Neighboring African countries, afraid that their own ethnic groups and regions might declare independence, were especially reluctant to recognize Somaliland.

In 2005 the TFG finally moved to Somalia, but members disagreed over where to meet. President Ahmed said Mogadishu was not safe. He and the prime minister set up offices in the town of Jawhar, about 56 miles (90 km) north of the capital. The speaker of the assembly and some other assembly members worked in Mogadishu, however. Meanwhile, the government had no real authority over the country.

Some observers worried that full-scale civil war would return. Outbreaks of violence continued, and someone tried to kill the vice president. Finally, the politicians reached a compromise. Members of the Transitional Federal Assembly held their first meeting on home soil in the city of Baydhabo. They voted to make this city the government's temporary base.

At the same time, the worst drought in many years created an emergency in Somalia. Crops withered and livestock died. Even the camels were skinny. There was only enough water for three cups per day per person, far too little in such a hot climate. Children and adults died of thirst and starvation.

Waters off the Somali coast became increasingly lawless in 2005. Pirates armed with automatic weapons threatened and hijacked cargo ships and ships delivering food to famine-stricken areas. Shipping companies started avoiding Somali ports. When pirates unsuccessfully attacked a cruise ship offshore, passenger vessels stopped sailing in Somali waters altogether. The transitional government hired a U.S. security company to help fight the ocean outlaws.

Foreign aid workers warned the world that more than one and a half million people were in danger of dying. International groups sent food by ship, but Somali pirates hijacked the ships. Armed militias also set up checkpoints along roads. When trucks came by with food shipments, militias forced the drivers to pay "taxes" to continue on the roads. What little aid reached the country often did not get to the people who needed it most. In addition, food aid programs were short on supplies and money.

Members of the international media were unable to travel to Somalia because it was too dangerous. As a result, most people around the world were unaware of the disaster. They left Somalia to sort out its own problems.

◉ The Islamic Courts Union

In 2006 Somalia again appeared in news stories around the world. This time, leaders of local Islamic courts formed a group called the Islamic Courts Union (ICU). The union acquired weapons and a militia and began fighting the warlords. Over several months of heavy fighting in Mogadishu, many people, including civilians (nonsoldiers), were killed or injured.

In June 2006, the ICU defeated the warlords and took control of Mogadishu. It then moved to take over other parts of Somalia. Many Somalis were happy. They hated the warlords because they had caused so much misery for so long. They hoped the Islamic Courts would bring peace, law, and order to the country. Other people worried that if the ICU formed a government, it would force people to follow a strict form of Islam. The United States also worried that the ICU had links to Islamist terrorists in other countries. Meanwhile, the TFG tried to keep the ICU from taking control of the whole country.

In the summer and fall of 2006, neighboring nations joined in the struggle over Somalia's future. Ethiopia sent troops to help the temporary

Residents of Jawhar **celebrate the defeat of warlords** by the Islamic Courts Union in June 2006.

government. Eritrea sent troops to help the ICU. In addition, nearby Islamic nations, including Iran, Libya, and Saudi Arabia, sent money and weapons to the ICU. By late 2006, Somalia was split between government and ICU forces. Warfare and lawlessness were on the rise, with little hope of peace or stability in sight.

Visit www.vgsbooks.com for links to websites with additional information about recent events in Somalia, including news stories and photographs.

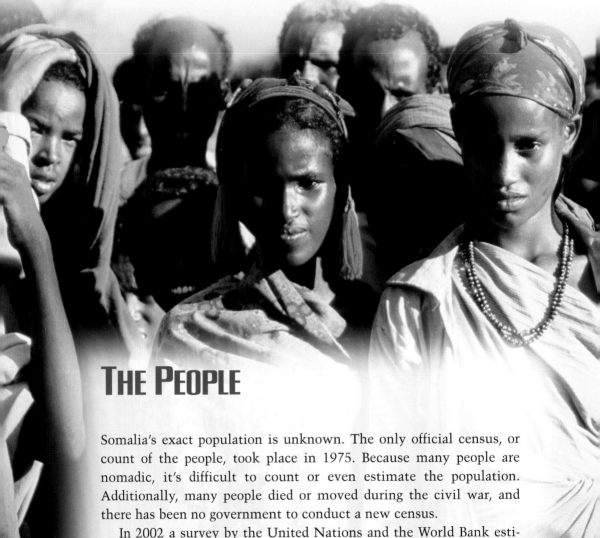

THE PEOPLE

Somalia's exact population is unknown. The only official census, or count of the people, took place in 1975. Because many people are nomadic, it's difficult to count or even estimate the population. Additionally, many people died or moved during the civil war, and there has been no government to conduct a new census.

In 2002 a survey by the United Nations and the World Bank estimated that 6.8 million people lived in Somalia. In 2003 the World Health Organization put the population at 9.9 million. The Population Reference Bureau (PRB) estimated that 8.6 million people lived in Somalia in mid-2005. (All these estimates include Somaliland's population.) The population density is estimated at 35 people per square mile (13 people per sq. km).

An estimated 400,000 people died during the civil war from violence, famine, or disease. The violence also forced 45 percent of the population to abandon their homes, at least temporarily. Some went to Europe or North America. Hundreds of thousands fled to camps in

nearby countries or simply moved elsewhere in Somalia.

Prior to the civil war, four out of five Somalis lived in the country-side or in small villages. But during the war, many families abandoned the farmland and animals that supplied their incomes. Many fled to cities. In 2005 the PRB estimated that one-third of Somalis were living in cities.

Health

Because of warfare, hunger, drought, and poor health care, life expectancy in Somalia is very low. At birth, a Somali male can expect to live just 46 years, and a Somali female 49 years. Only 3 percent of the population is over age 65, while 45 percent of Somalis are under age 15.

On average, each woman gives birth seven times in her lifetime. Less than 10 percent of married women use birth control. Because of the high birthrate, Somalia's population is growing quickly. Experts think it could grow to 25.5 million by 2050.

Somali women and children wait for food at a United Nations feeding center in southern Somalia. Somali children face a high death rate due to diseases such as malaria and respiratory infections.

Somalia has a high rate of infant mortality (numbers of children who die before their first birthdays), with 120 infant deaths out of every 1,000 births. Childhood mortality (death rates for children) is also high. Out of every 1,000 children, 224 die before they reach their fifth birthdays. The rate of maternal deaths (deaths of mothers from causes related to childbirth) is high as well, at 1,100 deaths per 100,000 births.

The high rate of maternal death stems from several factors. For one thing, the nation suffers from a shortage of doctors and nurses. Trained medical staff attend only one-third of births. Complicating matters, like many other African peoples, Somalis practice female genital mutilation (FGM). FGM involves the surgical removal of a girl's outer genitalia. Sometimes the vagina is sewn shut, leaving only a tiny opening. The stitching proves that a girl is a virgin when she marries. The procedure is usually done without painkillers and under unsanitary conditions. Infections are common. Some girls die, while others experience lifelong health and reproductive problems. (Some outsiders are fighting to end FGM in Somalia and other nations. But Somali society puts great pressure on families to continue the custom.)

Half of all Somalis have no access to sanitation facilities, such as toilets or running water. Some people dig latrines (pits in the ground) to use as toilets, while others just relieve themselves outside. Since Somalia has no government, it has no garbage collection. Waste simply piles up outdoors, attracting insects and animals that can spread disease.

Many people in Somalia don't have enough to eat, which makes them weak and sick. Eighty percent of Somalis have no access to safe drinking water. Unclean water spreads diseases such as hepatitis and typhoid fever. Without clean water to drink, people also die of dehydration.

Respiratory infections, such as coughs, are common, especially in crowded urban areas. Measles, cholera, and tetanus are also widespread. In the wet season, Somalia swarms with mosquitoes, which spread deadly diseases such as malaria and dengue fever. The World Health Organization estimated that 2 million cases of malaria occur in Somalia each year.

Somalia has one of the world's highest rates of tuberculosis (TB), a disease that damages the lungs and can lead to death. Tuberculosis is especially difficult to treat because a patient must take medicine regularly for months. In Somalia many TB patients cannot afford to buy medicine. Sometimes dishonest druggists even sell fake pills to TB patients.

No one knows how many people in Somalia are infected with the human immunodeficiency virus, or HIV. HIV is the virus that causes AIDS (acquired immunodeficiency syndrome). AIDS destroys the human immune system. Without treatment, most people with AIDS grow extremely sick and die. A 2001 estimate put the HIV rate in Somalia at 1 percent of the adult population. International health organizations are trying to treat Somalis with AIDS and to educate Somalis about HIV/AIDS prevention. But programs are not widespread or well funded.

In a country marked by frequent warfare, gunshot wounds are common, even among civilians. Every year, many people accidentally step on landmines. The resulting explosions can maim and kill victims.

LANDMINES

Warlords and their militias have placed up to one million landmines in Somalia, hiding the explosive devices near military bases, on grazing land, and near schools and water sources. One aid group estimated that landmines killed or wounded 3,500 victims in Somaliland in 1992, during the civil war. Even after the war, Somalia is still littered with mines. Dozens of people die from landmine explosions each year. Many people who survive landmine injuries are severely wounded *(below)* and never return to work. Some militia leaders have promised to dispose of their landmine stockpiles. The governments of Somaliland and Puntland have also promised to remove existing landmines.

Living in a violent and unpredictable environment can also cause stress and other mental health problems.

Most large towns and cities have hospitals and health centers. Organizations such the Somali Red Crescent Society (similar to the American Red Cross) and an international group called Doctors Without Borders run some health clinics in rural regions. But many Somalis still don't get health care. Sometimes, patients travel hundreds of miles to reach a hospital or clinic, only to find that it is in territory controlled by an enemy militia. In addition, many people cannot afford to pay for medical care. Many people die because they lack basic health care. People who are wounded during warfare often get no treatment.

Internally Displaced Persons

During the civil war, armed militias attacked villages, burned homes, and stole people's land. They tended to attack farmers, members of small or weak clans, and members of minority ethnic groups. The militias killed many victims and forced others to work as laborers on land that had previously belonged to them.

Still other victims fled their land when militias arrived. They left their homes to seek safety elsewhere. Although Mogadishu was the most dangerous place in the country, some 250,000 people fled there during the war, hoping to find work and medical care.

People who have relocated to other regions of Somalia are known as internally displaced persons (IDPs). Since 1991, hundreds of thou-

More than eight thousand **internally displaced persons live at the Maslah camp** in Waajid, Somalia. It is about 211 miles (340 km) west of Mogadishu.

sands of Somalis have become IDPs. Most IDPs were displaced before 1995. But even in the early 2000s, Somalis continued to flee when violence flared up in their communities. In 2005 the United Nations estimated that up to 400,000 Somalis remained displaced, with little hope of returning home in the near future.

Some IDPs live in makeshift camps run by international aid organizations. Most live in urban areas. They build huts out of rags, cardboard, plastic, and sticks, or they live in abandoned public buildings. Some survive by begging. Others take any job they can find. Many child IDPs work to help support their families. Most IDPs cannot afford to eat more than once a day. Most have no access to clean water, health care, or education.

Female IDPs are especially vulnerable. Attackers sometimes rape women and girls in their flimsy huts, which offer little protection. Other times, attackers rape women and girls when they leave their homes to haul water from wells. Enemies also sometimes assault female IDPs to humiliate their husbands.

Ethnic Groups

About 85 percent of the people of Somalia belong to one ethnic group, the Somali. They are related to the Oromo, who make up a large percentage of the population of Ethiopia. They are also related to ethnic groups in nearby Djibouti, Sudan, and Kenya. The remaining 15 percent of the population belongs

SOMALIS AROUND THE WORLD

In the nineteenth century, some Somali sailors worked on British ships. Some of them settled in London, England, and elsewhere. In the 1920s, some Somali immigrants settled in New York City in the United States. In the 1960s, many Somalis went to the United States and other Western countries to attend college. Afterward, they returned to their newly independent homeland. A decade later, many more Somalis crossed the Gulf of Aden to work in the oil industry on the Arabian Peninsula.

During the civil war, hundreds of thousands of Somalis left their nation for Europe, the United States, Canada, and Australia. In modern times, more than one million Somalis live in communities scattered around the world. Many of them send money to relatives back in Africa. This money is crucial to Somalia's economy.

In the United States, Somali refugees form one of the largest African immigrant groups. In their new home, Somalis try to adapt, learn English, attend school, and get jobs. Most Somalis in the United States practice the Muslim religion and eat traditional Somali foods.

THE DIYA-PAYING GROUP

The *diya*-paying group was an important element of Somali society, especially in the past. It was made up of one hundred or more closely related families within a clan. If someone killed or injured someone else, the other members of the culprit's diya group had to pay up to one hundred camels (the diya, or payment) to the injured party's group. This system helped reduce conflict and violence, but sometimes groups still fought with each other. To create national unity, President Siad Barre tried to eliminate diya-paying groups, but they did not disappear. In recent years, diya-paying groups have played a role in maintaining law and order, especially in rural areas.

to other ethnic groups, mainly the Bantu-language group. Bantu speakers are related to the people of central and southern Africa. A tiny fraction of Somalia's people are of Arab descent. Ethnic Somalis are found throughout the country, while Bantu speakers tend to live in the riverine region. Arab Somalis primarily live in the coastal cities.

Each Somali person is also a member of a clan. Clan members trace their family histories many generations back, from father to father. Clan membership is the foundation of each person's identity. For instance, when two Somalis meet, they don't ask, Where are you from? or What do you do for a living? They ask, Whom are you from? In other words, What clan do you belong to?

The four main clans are the Dir, the Darod, the Isaaq, and the Hawiye. The Dir come from northwestern Somaliland and nearby regions of Ethiopia and Djibouti. The Isaaq dominate Somaliland. The Darod are primarily from Puntland, or northeastern Somalia. The Hawiye live in central Somalia and Mogadishu. Smaller clans, the Digil and Rahanwayn, are based in the riverine region of southern Somalia.

Members of the same clan often help one another, for instance by giving each other jobs or protecting each other from enemies. But bitter clan rivalries have helped divide Somalia. Clans and smaller subclans continuously make and break alliances with each other. The civil war was marked by clans fighting one another.

Education and Literacy

Everyone in Somalia speaks the Somali language. However, during much of the twentieth century, English and Italian were used in schools and government. Before independence, only 5 percent of Somalis were literate (able to read and write).

The government improved education during the early years of independence. By 1980, Somalia had about 1,400 elementary schools. Education was free. After high school, many students attended vocational (job-training) schools or the National University of Somalia in Mogadishu. Outstanding students obtained scholarships (financial assistance) to study in Europe, the Soviet Union, the Middle East, or China. By 1990 the United Nations estimated that about 24 percent of Somalis could read and write.

But education went into steep decline during the civil war. Warfare damaged or destroyed about 90 percent of the nation's schools. Most children who grew up during the 1990s received no education at all. After the war, the few school buildings left standing became living quarters for homeless families or headquarters for local militias.

By the early 2000s, Somalia had one of the lowest school enrollment rates in the world. In 2002, just 17 percent of children (21 percent of boys and 13 percent of girls) were enrolled in elementary school. The literacy rate stood at about 19 percent.

In relatively safe areas, such as Puntland, aid organizations are helping rebuild public schools. But the nation still suffers from a shortage of teachers, textbooks, supplies, and classrooms. A few wealthy families send their children to private schools. Many families send their children to Quranic schools, where students study Arabic and the Quran, Islam's holy book. Quranic schools usually charge low fees because classes are held in tents, or students sit outside in the shade of a large tree.

A girl studies Arabic at a Quranic school in Baydhabo.

HOUSES

Houses vary in Somalia, depending on the location. On the coast, people build with coral, limestone, and concrete. In interior areas, people build wooden houses with roofs made of metal or thatch (a mat of grasses and other plants). In the north, people build their homes from sun-dried bricks.

Nomads live in dome-shaped dwellings called *aqals*. Aqals *(below)* are made of poles arranged in a semicircle and covered with thatch. Sometimes people use animal hides, empty grain sacks, and pieces of plastic to make the walls. They hang household goods, such as baskets and utensils, from hooks on the walls. They cook outside. When nomads move to a new place, they take apart their aqals and load them onto camels. Women are responsible for building and taking down aqals and for keeping them in good condition.

Bullets and bombs destroyed the National University of Somalia. To replace it, private donors founded Mogadishu University in 1997. With a new campus on the outskirts of Mogadishu, the school offers classes in nursing, economics, computer science, education, and other fields. Several other small universities have recently been established in Somalia and Somaliland.

◉ Women and Families

The traditional role of women in Somalia is to cook, clean, and care for children. According to Islamic law, a Somali man can have up to four wives at once, as long as he can sup-

port them. About one in five Somali men has more than one wife. Usually, each wife has her own residence and looks after her own children. Many Somali women are influential in family decisions. But women do not play important roles in business or government in Somalia. In the countryside, families sometimes arrange for their young daughters to marry much older men. In the cities, many young people choose their own marriage partners, however.

The civil war affected many families. Thousands of men were killed. Others suffered injuries that left them unable to work. Families were often separated when the women and children moved into camps for refugees (people who flee their homes to escape danger). Without husbands to help them, many Somali women support their children by selling cloth, milk, or other items at local markets.

Visit www.vgsbooks.com for links to websites with additional information about the Somali culture. Learn about the different ethnic groups and Somalis living in foreign countries.

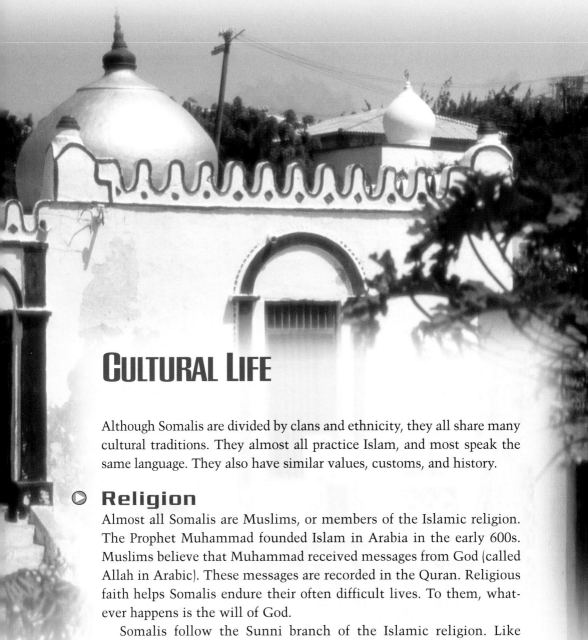

CULTURAL LIFE

Although Somalis are divided by clans and ethnicity, they all share many cultural traditions. They almost all practice Islam, and most speak the same language. They also have similar values, customs, and history.

◉ Religion

Almost all Somalis are Muslims, or members of the Islamic religion. The Prophet Muhammad founded Islam in Arabia in the early 600s. Muslims believe that Muhammad received messages from God (called Allah in Arabic). These messages are recorded in the Quran. Religious faith helps Somalis endure their often difficult lives. To them, whatever happens is the will of God.

Somalis follow the Sunni branch of the Islamic religion. Like Muslims everywhere, devout Somalis follow practices called the Five Pillars of Islam. All Muslims are supposed to: (1) proclaim their belief in Allah and Allah's prophet, Muhammad; (2) say prayers five times a day; (3) take no food or water between sunrise and sunset

during the holy month of Ramadan; (4) give charity to the poor; and (5) make a pilgrimage (a trip to a sacred place) to the holy city of Mecca in Saudi Arabia at least once a lifetime, if possible. Many Somalis are unable to fulfill the last two requirements because they are too poor.

Every Somali town has a mosque where people can worship. Since nomads travel across the countryside, where there are no mosques, traveling religious teachers lead prayers, perform marriage ceremonies, bless livestock, and try to resolve disputes for nomads.

Some Somalis practice a mystical form of Islam called Sufism, which came to Somalia from Arabia in the 1400s. Somali Sufis sometimes visit the tombs of nineteenth-century Sufi leaders in southern Somalia. Some Somali men join Sufi brotherhoods called *tariqas*. Tariqa members try to develop closer relationships with God by living simple lives. They try to achieve higher spiritual states by chanting or going into trances. Many Somalis believe that tariqa leaders are blessed. But other Somalis reject Sufism as superstition. They follow a stricter approach to Islam.

The influence of Islamic groups has slowly increased in Somali society. Some modern Islamic groups provide health care and education in their communities. In many communities, Islamic leaders enforce law and order through sharia courts. Court leaders base their rulings on the teachings of the Quran and the hadith, the sayings and deeds of the prophet Muhammad. In 2006 leaders of sharia courts joined forces to form the Islamic Courts Union. Their well-armed militias defeated the warlords of Mogadishu.

The Somali Language

Somali is the country's official language. Almost all Somalis speak Somali, although there are several different dialects, or versions, of the language. For example, members of the Digil and Rahanwayn clans speak a dialect that is quite distinct from the language that most Somalis use. Somali is related to languages spoken in Ethiopia, Djibouti, and Nigeria. It is distantly related to the Middle Eastern languages of Arabic and Hebrew. Many Somali people speak Arabic in addition to Somali, and the Somali language includes many words borrowed from Arabic. Some educated Somalis also speak English or Italian.

For thousands of years, there was no written form of Somali. When Arabs and Europeans arrived in Somalia, they brought their languages and alphabets with them. For many years, people fought over which alphabet to use to write the Somali language. In 1972 the government decided to use the Roman alphabet, the same lettering system used to write English and other European languages.

Poetry

Somalis are famous for their skills as poets. In fact, poetry is almost as important as the Islamic faith in Somali culture. Skilled poets are highly regarded.

Some poems are simple verses that deal with ordinary, daily tasks. Other poems are more elaborate discussions about culture and politics. Somali poetry is full of metaphors, or symbols. For example, a camel might stand for beauty, women, food, or Somalia's political independence.

In writing Somali poetry, people must follow strict rules. Each line must have a certain numbers of syllables and a certain pattern of vowels. Certain words in each line must share the same first letter. Poems are often put to music.

Poems are also often put to political uses. For instance, prior to the civil war, the government used state-owned radio to broadcast poems that defended government policies. Some modern poems criticize politicians or warlords.

Poetry in Somalia is primarily a speaking and listening experience. Very few poetry books have been published. Nomadic families often sit around bonfires at night to recite and listen to stories and poetry. In towns, men gather at local teashops to listen to poets. Somalis also hold poetry competitions that can last for days or weeks. During a competition, everyone in a village will gather in the shade under acacia trees to hear poets recite their works. With each round of the competition, the poets try to outdo each other. Elders serve as judges, evaluating competitors on their talent. Winners get prizes of livestock, as well as fame and honor for their clans.

Camels are the subjects of many poems, songs, and stories, and there are many words in the Somali language to describe them. For example, *awr* is a male camel used to carry things. *Irmaan* is a dairy camel. *Mandhoorey* means the best camel in the herd. *Baloolley* refers to a female camel that may or may not give milk, depending on her mood.

Mohamed Ibrahim Warsame Hadrawi is a well-known modern-day poet. He has written several volumes of poetry, written and directed plays, and composed some of the most popular Somali songs.

Stories and Theater

Since ancient times, Somalis have enjoyed listening to storytellers. Some stories recount clan history, and many are Arab in origin. Igall Bowkahh is a favorite character in folktales. He is a humorous person who survives by being tough and stubborn. Some Somalis write novels. One of them is Faarax M. J. Cawl. His 1974 novel *Ignorance Is the Enemy of Love* tells the story of an illiterate warrior. He is unable to read a letter from the girl who loves him, with tragic results.

Somalis love theater. When a traveling troupe of actors comes to a town, everyone attends the performance. Plays are usually written in verse and include both comedy and music. While entertaining, the plots generally deal with social issues and impart lessons about right and wrong.

Music

Music is another important part of Somali life. Musical styles range from traditional work songs to modern-style jazz. In Mogadishu, musicians have incorporated African, Arabic, and Indian rhythms into their compositions. Somalis love to listen to the radio and share cassette

The **Somali National Theater Company** performs in traditional costumes.

recordings with their friends. Somalis also enjoy folk dancing at weddings and on holidays.

In earlier eras, Somali music consisted mainly of singing, often accompanied by clapping, drumming, and simple reed flutes. In the twentieth century, musicians added stringed instruments such as the *kaban*, which resembles a four-stringed guitar, and the oud, an Arab-style lute. But the human voice is the central element of Somali music, and many songs have no accompaniment. People sing romantic love ballads, songs about cheating husbands, and songs that denounce corrupt politicians.

Abdi Badil is a singer and kaban player who rose to fame in the early 1980s when he won a radio talent competition. Abdulkadir Jubba's lively songs are popular at weddings. Many of his fans know the words to his songs by heart. Maryam Mursal, who lives in Denmark, began her singing career in 1966 and then became the most famous female star in her homeland. She sings both traditional Somali music and a mixture of Western and African sounds known as Somali jazz.

Clothing and Weaving

Somali clothing is a mix of old and new styles. In the countryside, men sometimes wear a long cloth called a *futa*. It is wrapped around the waist like a long skirt. In urban areas, men often wear modern shirts and trousers, similar to clothes worn by men in the United States.

Women's clothes also come in a variety of styles, both traditional and modern. Women sometimes wear full-length traditional dresses called *guntiinos*. They are made of long pieces of elaborately wrapped and brightly colored cloth. More common is a loose dress called a *diri*.

Women like to decorate their hands and feet with vegetable dyes for special occasions, such as weddings. In recent years, as a stricter form of Islam has become more prominent in Somalia, many women have started to wear head scarves and veils, an Islamic custom.

Southern cities such as Mogadishu were once famous for their white cloth, handwoven from cotton grown in the riverine region. Some weavers dyed their cloth with vegetable dyes, creating elaborate patterns. Prior to the civil war, designers made Somali cloth into modern, Western-style fashions, sold in fancy Mogadishu shops. The civil war put an end to this business. In modern times, traditional weaving is a dying art. Foreign, factory-made cloth is so inexpensive that weavers find it hard to sell handmade products. In addition, many weavers were killed or became refugees during the war.

CRAFTS

Somali nomads keep their possessions to a minimum because they have to carry them wherever they go. But many practical items are very beautiful. Wooden milk vessels, for example, are carved with intricate geometric patterns. Somalis also carve wooden spoons and walking sticks. They make leather stools and bags, bells for camels, and gold jewelry. While carving is a man's responsibility, some women are expert basket makers. They weave grasses into containers that are tight enough to carry liquids.

Food

Somali food incorporates the cuisines of East Africa, India, and Arabia, with an added dash of Italian flavors. Meat and milk form the basis of the Somali diet. Women cook goat, beef, or lamb by grilling, broiling, or frying it in ghee (a type of liquid butter). They season the meat with spices such as turmeric, coriander, and cumin. Spaghetti with meat sauce and goat meat stew are popular dishes. *Sambusas*, or spicy meat dumplings, are favorites at weddings and feasts. Camel meat is not a popular food, but nomads often take *otka*, or dried camel meat, on long trips, since it keeps well.

Both children and adults drink milk. Although they do drink milk from cows and goats, Somalis prefer camel milk. Other common foods include rice, sorghum (a type of grain), dates, and fruit such as bananas, grapefruit, papayas, and mangoes. People who live near the coast eat fresh fish. Bread, made with various types of flour, is extremely popular. *Canjeero* is a type of flatbread. *Soor* is a porridge made with sorghum.

Somalis love tea. They make it very sweet and spicy. Some people put milk or lemon in their tea. In villages, men gather, talk, and drink tea at

Two Somali men enjoy some tea at a nomad camp.

SOMALI SPICED TEA

Drinking sweet and spicy tea is an old tradition in Somalia. Somali men sit for hours in tea houses, where they drink tea and chat.

4 cups water

3 teabags black tea

4 whole cardamom pods

4 whole cloves

1 stick cinnamon

milk and sugar, to taste

1. In a kettle or saucepan, bring the water to a boil.
2. Add the tea and spices. Allow to sit for 4–5 minutes. Strain before serving.

Tea may be served with or without milk and sugar.

Serves six

small teashops. People also buy tea from stalls along the street or from tea sellers pushing wheelbarrows crammed with bottles of hot tea.

Sports and Games

In peaceful areas of the country, Somalis enjoy sports such as table tennis, running, and basketball. They especially love soccer, which they play in local leagues. But the country lacks the facilities and equipment to develop world-class athletes. There are few opportunities for girls to play sports.

Shax, also known as *jar*, is a popular Somali game, played by men only. Elderly nomads and unemployed young men may spend hours outdoors, playing shax on game squares drawn in the dirt, while observers watch and comment. In this game of strategy, each of two players has twelve game pieces, which he moves around the board, trying to line up three in a row.

Boys and girls enjoy *girir*, a game played with small stones and a hole in the ground. Each player tosses a stone in the air and catches it again while moving other stones in and out of the hole.

Holidays and Festivals

Most holidays celebrated in Somalia are associated with Islam. Their dates vary according to the lunar calendar, a calendar determined by the movements of the moon rather than the sun. During the holy month of Ramadan, Muslims must fast (take no food or water) during daylight. Eid al-Fitr (Feast of the Fast Breaking) is a three-day celebration at the end of Ramadan. At this time, people eat, pray, exchange presents, and wear new clothes.

Eid al-Adha (Feast of the Sacrifice) honors the prophet Abraham's obedience to God. This celebration coincides with the hajj, the annual pilgrimage to Mecca. All Muslims try to make this journey at least once in their lives. Mawlid al-Nabi is the birthday of the Prophet Muhammed, while Mi'raaj al-Nabi is the day on which the prophet ascended to heaven.

The *gu* rainy season, when food and water are plenty, is often a time for special occasions, such as weddings and poetry competitions. People also offer sacrifices, or gifts, to Allah during this season. An individual's age is calculated by the number of gu seasons he or she has lived through.

Dab-shid, the Festival of Fire, marks the beginning of the farming season. It falls at the end of July. During this festival, people build bonfires and splash water around. In some communities, they perform dances and stick fights.

People in Somaliland observe additional holidays. They celebrate Labor Day on May 1, the restoration of Somaliland's independence from Somalia on May 18–19, and Independence Day (from the British) on June 26.

Visit www.vgsbooks.com for links to websites with additional information about Somali culture, including holidays, foods, sports, and games.

THE ECONOMY

Somalia is one of the poorest nations in the world, with an average income per person of $226 a year. About 43 percent of Somalis live in extreme poverty, defined as living on less than one U.S. dollar per day. The overall unemployment rate is 47 percent. Unemployment is highest in urban areas, where 62 percent of eligible workers don't have jobs.

Even prior to the civil war, Somalia had low levels of education, few industries, and low incomes. Following the government's collapse in 1991, government employees and teachers lost their jobs, and the few existing factories closed. Many family breadwinners were injured, killed, or separated from their families during the war. Farmers had to flee their land and livestock. The economy fell into shambles.

Most Somalis with skills and education left the country, making the rebuilding of the nation's economy even more challenging. Warlords controlled roads, ports, and airports so they could collect

money from users. They also controlled city neighborhoods. Warlords had no interest in working for the common good. They did not want a centralized government because they prospered without one.

After the fighting calmed down, a few Somalis managed to open businesses. They usually worked with members of their own clans, since these are people they feel they can trust. Some businesspeople started telephone services, sugar refineries, and soft-drink-bottling factories.

Somalia's estimated gross domestic product (GDP—the value of all goods and services produced in the nation in one year) was $4.8 billion in 2005. To understand how low this figure is, consider that neighboring Kenya had a GDP of $37 billion in 2005. Agriculture represents about 65 percent of Somalia's GDP. Industry accounts for 10 percent, and services (communications, health care, government work, and sales) account for 25 percent.

A VALUABLE BEAST

Somalis regard livestock as a source of wealth, and the camel is the most valuable animal of every herd. When a couple marries, the groom's family often gives the bride's family camels. Camels are a source of milk, wool, and hides. They can also carry heavy burdens. Even camel dung is useful. It can be burned as fuel.

The camels of Somalia are dromedaries—camels with one fat-filled hump. A 1989 study estimated that there were more than six million camels in Somalia, about half of all the camels in Africa. Camels eat desert shrubs that other animals ignore, and they can survive for long periods without water. In the dry season, a camel needs to drink once every ten to twenty days, while sheep and goats need water every three to eight days, and cattle every two or three days.

Camels are valuable animals in Somalia. A Somali nomad girl leads camels carrying her family's possessions.

◉ Sources of Income

Agriculture—including fishing, growing crops, and raising livestock—accounts for 71 percent of employment in Somalia. Industry, including construction and manufacturing, and services, such as jobs in restaurants and stores, make up 29 percent of employment.

Fifty percent of people's income comes from self-employment, such as a family raising and selling its own livestock. Wage employment (working for someone else for a set rate of pay) accounts for 14 percent of income. Remittances, or money sent from relatives living in other countries, represent 22 percent of income. The remaining 14 percent comes from other sources, such as renting out property.

Income levels vary in different parts of the country. Prior to the war, some people worked at well-paying industrial jobs in

Mogadishu and other cities. The fertile south was also a fairly wealthy area. Since the war died down, the areas with the highest income levels have been the regions with the least fighting.

Livestock

Livestock herding is the backbone of the Somali economy and culture. Fifty-five per cent of Somalis depend on livestock for their income. Even many city residents own a few animals, although relatives who live in the countryside care for them.

A 1988 study found an estimated 19.4 million goats, 10.8 million black-headed sheep, 6.2 million camels, and 4.6 million cattle in Somalia. Goats are easy to raise because they eat almost anything. Sheep can eat coarse grass. Cattle need to drink water more frequently than sheep and goats. Cattle are primarily found in the south, which is wetter than the north.

Somali herders eat meat and milk produced by their livestock, but they primarily raise animals to sell for cash. Livestock has always been Somalia's most important export product. Traders buy animals and put them on ships bound for the Arabian Peninsula. Traders also walk or truck livestock to market in Kenya.

The livestock sector faces serious difficulties, however. Livestock sales fell in 2000 when Saudi Arabia refused to buy livestock from the Horn of Africa, saying the animals carried disease. This situation is linked to Somalia's political problems. During the war, veterinarians left the country, and veterinary training schools closed. There is no government department to keep an eye on disease outbreaks, vaccinate animals to prevent disease, or teach herders modern breeding methods.

Crop Production

Twenty-five percent of Somalis support themselves by growing and selling crops. Some farmers grow crops and also raise livestock. Vegetable crops include onions, carrots, corn, and peppers. Farmers in the riverine region grow bananas, grapefruit, limes, papayas, and mangoes. Other farmers grow sugarcane, sorghum, and tomatoes.

Somali farmers face many difficulties. In recent years, floods and droughts have damaged plants. Warfare has destroyed irrigation systems and disrupted farming. Even in peaceful areas, Somali farmers have trouble getting seeds that will grow well in Somalia's hot climate. To improve crop production, farmers must use chemical fertilizers (which help plants grow) and pesticides (which kill insects), but these products can be dangerous to human health. Farmers also lack training in farming techniques. They don't have good irrigation equipment or refrigerators for storing crops. Bad roads make it difficult to transport produce to the cities.

FRANKINCENSE AND MYRRH

Myrrh comes from several species of *Commiphora*, fragrant small trees or shrubs with short, thorny branches. These plants grow in Africa and the Middle East, including the northern mountain slopes of Somalia. To harvest myrrh, workers make slits in a plant's bark. A substance called resin oozes out. Exposed to the air, it hardens and turns reddish brown. Myrrh has been used since ancient times as incense and perfume, and as a medicine and dressing for wounds. People in China still use it to treat wounds and relieve pain. Somalia is a major source of myrrh for the Chinese market.

Frankincense comes from several species of *Boswellia* trees, commonly found on the mountainsides of Somalia, as well as in Yemen and Oman. Workers also get frankincense through cuts in the tree bark. The milky liquid that oozes from the cuts hardens in the air. The ancient Egyptians used frankincense in religious rituals. Throughout history, people have also used frankincense to treat various ailments, but modern scientists do not believe it has medicinal value. It is still used in incense and perfumes.

Militias often put up roadblocks on highways and demand money from truck drivers transporting goods. Furthermore, many city residents are so poor that they cannot afford to buy fruits and vegetables from farmers.

◉ Trade

Because it has no government, Somalia does not have official relations with other countries. But this situation has not stopped businesspeople from making deals with foreign buyers and sellers. Exports from Somalia were worth an estimated $241 million in 2004. Exported products include livestock, animal hides and skins, sugar, sorghum, and corn. The main buyers were the United Arab Emirates, Thailand, Yemen, and Oman.

Imports (products purchased from abroad) come from Djibouti, Kenya, Brazil, Saudi Arabia, and India. They include manufactured items, fuel oil, food, and construction materials. Imports were worth an estimated $576 million in 2004.

Currency traders do business in city markets, with piles of U.S. dollars and Somali shillings, as well as Kenyan and Ethiopian money, stacked on tables in front of them. They exchange one type of money for the other so that Somalis can do business with people in other countries.

Remittances are a mainstay of the Somali economy and were worth an estimated $800 million to $1 billion in 2004. Somalia hasn't had a government-owned bank since 1991, so an unofficial banking system handles remittances. To a great extent, the system depends on trust. Somalis living abroad who want to send money to relatives give the money to Somali business agents in the cities where they live. The sender identifies the person to receive the money by describing his or her clan and relatives. The agent then transmits an order by fax or telephone to an office in Somalia. The recipient goes to the office and proves his or her identity by naming clan ancestors and relatives, then picks up the money. The remittance company takes a small percentage of the money as payment for handling the transaction.

This system functions well for honest Somalis. However, some people suspect that terrorist groups also use it to transfer money. Shortly after the al-Qaeda terrorist attacks against the United States in September 2001, the U.S. government forced the largest Somali remittance company to shut its offices.

KHAT ADDICTION

Khat chewing has become a serious problem in Somalia. Many people—mostly men—chew the leaves of the *Catha edulis* plant, nicknamed khat. The leaves contain a mild stimulant, a chemical that temporarily makes people feel active and alert. Over the long term, however, chewing khat makes users tired, depressed, and aggressive.

Khat arrives by the truckload from the highlands of Ethiopia, where the plant grows. Sellers load up carts and wheelbarrows and sell plastic bags full of khat. A growing number of heavy users spend their money on khat rather than supporting their families or investing in business or property.

Two **Somali currency traders** stand behind a counter at a store in the Bakara market in Mogadishu. Somali shillings are piled on the counter.

◉ Transportation

In Somali cities, some people own cars and other vehicles. In the countryside, people are more likely to travel on foot and to transport goods by loading them onto the backs of donkeys or camels. For public transportation, some people ride in taxis and buses. But the most common vehicles for public transportation are pickup trucks, with their beds crammed with passengers.

Somalia has an estimated 13,700 miles (22,000 km) of roads, about 12 percent of which are paved. Somaliland has 520 miles (840 km) of paved roads, connecting large centers such as Berbera and Hargeysa. Many unpaved roads turn to mud during the rainy season.

There are airports at Mogadishu, Baydhabo, and several other cities. Damal Airlines serves eight cities in Somalia and Somaliland. Several airports in Somaliland were damaged during the 1988 attack. As a result, the airports lack terminal buildings, air-traffic-control towers, and passenger services. Nevertheless, several airlines provide service from Somaliland to destinations such as

BERBERA: AN IMPORTANT PORT

Berbera (below) is the only deepwater port on the Gulf of Aden coast. Seven medium-sized ships can tie up at its wharf at one time. But most of the port's facilities were damaged during the civil war. The port's business outlook improved in 2005, when Ethiopian and Somaliland officials agreed that Berbera would handle a significant portion of landlocked Ethiopia's imports and exports. Local residents hope that Berbera will become an economic engine for the region.

Djibouti, Dubai, and Nairobi. Shipping cargo by air is a booming business in Somaliland.

Energy

Facilities to produce and distribute electricity were destroyed during the civil war. As a result, few Somali homes have electricity, especially outside the cities. Before the civil war, Somalia planned to build a hydroelectric dam on the Jubba River. The dam would have produced electricity from the power of flowing water. But the project was delayed by the war. A proposal to produce wind-generated power is also on hold. In the future, Somalis hope to use solar (sun) power to create electricity and to run irrigation and drinking water systems.

Media and Communications

Telephone service is one field where Somalia has had some success. The nation's public telephone system was destroyed during the civil war. But afterward, competing companies began offering phone services. There were an estimated 100,000 landline phones and 35,000 cell phones in Somalia in 2002, and calling rates were the lowest in Africa. Somalis also communicate with each other by mail. Private messenger services deliver letters and parcels.

Somalis love the radio. Often, a small group of nomads will sit around a battery-operated radio, listening to news or poetry. The nation's first radio station began broadcasting in Hargeysa in 1943, and a Mogadishu station opened in 1951. Some Somali radio stations broadcast only Somali news, music, and shows. As a result, songs that are big hits around the world are almost unknown in Somalia. Many people listen to Somali-language broadcasts of the BBC, the British radio network.

In the late 1990s, a privately owned television station began operations in Mogadishu, and another opened in Hargeysa. A government-owned station also operates in Hargeysa. But few Somalis have electricity or television sets in their homes. Only about 8 percent of Somalis in urban areas watch television, videos, or DVDs regularly. Some city restaurants have television sets, often tuned to news, talk, or African music programs. Very few Somalis have computers, and less than 1 percent of Somalis use the Internet.

During President Siad Barre's rule, the government owned the country's only newspaper. In recent years, a variety of newspapers and small news sheets have appeared in major cities. These papers allow readers to learn about different points of view. Somaliland has three widely distributed newspapers, one of which is government owned.

Somaliland: A Struggling Economy

When Siad Barre's forces attacked northern Somalia in 1988, most civilians fled to Ethiopia. When they began to return to the newly independent Somaliland a few years later, they found their homes and businesses destroyed. Nevertheless, herders rebuilt their livestock herds. Other people started small businesses.

Livestock is Somaliland's main source of income. The region's entire economy suffers when problems arise in the livestock industry, such as overgrazing or too little rainfall. The ban on livestock exports from the Horn of Africa to Saudi Arabia has had a devastating impact in Somaliland.

Besides livestock, Somaliland's other exports include animal hides and skins, and frankincense and myrrh, exported mainly to Djibouti. Imports include foods such as rice, sugar, and flour, as well as clothing, fuel, building materials, machinery, vehicles, and chemicals.

Typical small businesses include restaurants, construction companies, retail shops, and taxi services. But running a small business in Somaliland isn't easy. Many business owners lack management and accounting skills. People who want to open or expand businesses have to find private sources of funds, since there are no banks to lend them money. Some people sell livestock to raise funds. Others use remittance money.

 At www.vgsbooks.com, you'll find links to the latest information on the Somali economy, in addition to a converter where you can see the current exchange rate and convert U.S. dollars into Somali shillings.

The Future

In 2006, more than fifteen years after the civil war began, Somalia was neither at peace nor at war. The Transitional Federal Government had accomplished little and had no control over the country. For the most part, community life continued under the guidance of clan elders and Islamic religious leaders. Meanwhile, occasional outbreaks of violence occurred, especially in the capital. The Islamic Courts Union took advantage of the government's weakness and the unpopularity of the warlords. Its militia took firm control—first of the capital, then of other parts of the country.

Many Somalis yearn for order in their lives. Most observers agree that the restoration of peace and security should be Somalia's top priority.

This means guns must be removed from the streets. This process will not be easy after so many years of violence. In addition, Somalis are independent-minded people whose traditional loyalty is to family and clan. They do not have a long history of centralized government. Their most recent government was led by a dictator who caused Somalia more harm than good.

Neighboring countries have helped with the peace process, but Somalis have to do the hard work themselves. Somalis do not want foreigners on their soil, even to enforce peace. In recent years, several foreign aid workers and journalists have been kidnapped or killed there.

If and when Somalis find the political stability to rebuild their shattered country, foreign observers say the government will need more than $1 billion for the first two years of reconstruction. Meanwhile, the country already owes foreign lenders more than $2.8 billion.

On the positive side, Somalia has shown that people can organize themselves at the community level by running small businesses, Islamic courts, and Islamic schools. But while there have been some success stories, most Somalis have suffered, especially because of the lack of health care and education.

If Somalia is to find peace and stability, the country must disarm approximately 55,000 militiamen who have little education and few job skills. These men need to learn to support themselves as carpenters, engineers, and so on. The nation needs to rebuild its health care, police, transportation, water supply, sanitation, and other public services. The ruined capital needs to be reconstructed, and new jobs created. Somalis will also have to determine how to feed their growing population in a harsh environment.

Under the traditional clan system, fellow clan members helped one another with jobs and protection from enemies. But so many people have been displaced by war that the clan map of Somalia has been redrawn. The old social support system is gone. The future Somali government must help resettle IDPs and help create new social support networks. The government will also need to restore land to farmers who had property stolen during the war.

Another pressing issue is the future of the Republic of Somaliland. It is determined to remain independent of Somalia. But leaders of other countries, in Africa and abroad, want it to reunite with the south. This issue has the potential to reignite violence if Somalia tries to force the north into an unwanted reunion.

In short, the problems facing Somalia are many, and the solutions are not clear. It will likely take many years to bring peace and stability to this troubled country.

Timeline

CA. 2200 B.C. Travelers and traders from ancient Egypt visit the Land of Punt, which might have included modern-day Somalia.

300s B.C. Ancient Greeks begin to trade with people in Punt.

A.D. 700s People from Arabia and Persia establish settlements along the Somali coast.

900s Arab settlers establish Mogadishu on the Somali coast.

1000s Arab settlers introduce Islam to Somalia. The Arab sheik Daarood Jabarti marries the daughter of a Somali chief. His descendents are members of the Darod clan.

1200s Northern Somali clans begin to move southward.

EARLY 1400s Led by the sultan of Ifat, Haq ad-din, Somali Muslims battle Christians in neighboring Ethiopia.

1415 The word *Somali* appears in writing for the first time, in an Ethiopian hymn written to celebrate a victory against the Somalis.

1499–1518 Portuguese expeditions attack Somali coastal towns.

EARLY 1500s Led by Ahmed Guray, Somali Muslims again invade Ethiopia. Ethiopians enlist the help of Portuguese forces to fight the invaders.

1543 Ahmed Guray is killed in battle. The war ends with Ethiopia victorious.

1854 British explorer Richard Burton sails from Aden in Yemen, where the British have a coaling station, to Saylac. He then travels to Harer in modern-day Ethiopia.

1869 The Suez Canal, linking the Mediterranean and Red seas, opens.

1897 The homeland of the Somali people is split between British Somaliland, French Somaliland, and Italian Somaliland.

EARLY 1900s Mahammad Abdille Hasan (called the Mad Mullah) leads the Dervishes against the British.

1920 The Mad Mullah dies and the Dervish revolt collapses.

1939 World War II begins in Europe. The British and the Italians, who are enemies during the war, fight for control of Ethiopia and Somaliland.

1943 Somalis form the Somali Youth Club, a party working for Somali independence.

1945 World War II ends with a victory for Britain and its allies, leaving questions about future control of Somalia.

1949 The United Nations sets a timetable for independence for southern Somalia.

1960   North and south are united, and Somalia becomes an independent republic.

1969   General Mohamed Siad Barre and other military officers overthrow the government. Siad Barre dissolves the National Assembly and renames the country the Somali Democratic Republic.

1970   Siad Barre declares that Somalia will follow an economic policy called Scientific Socialism.

1973-74   The government teaches many Somalis to read and write.

1974   The government moves thousands of Somali nomads from the north to agricultural and fishing communities in the south.

1976   The former Soviet Union becomes Somalia's most important ally.

EARLY 1980S   Opponents of Siad Barre's government attack Somalia from Ethiopia.

LATE 1980S   The Somali National Movement attacks government forces in the north.

1988   Government forces bomb and destroy much of Hargeysa.

1989   Government forces attack members of the Hawiye clan in Mogadishu.

1991   Opponents overthrow Siad Barre, forcing him out of Mogadishu. Civil war follows. The Somali National Movement declares the formation of the Republic of Somaliland.

1992   Famine grips Somalia. The United States launches Operation Restore Hope to help restore peace and to make sure food aid reaches starving people.

1993   The United Nations takes over peacekeeping operations in Somalia. A U.S. Marine Corps helicopter is shot down in Mogadishu. A gunfight in the city streets results in the deaths of eighteen U.S. troops and more than three hundred Somalis.

1995   United Nations personnel withdraw from Somalia.

1998   Puntland breaks with Somalia and becomes a self-governing territory.

2000   Somali politicians, meeting in Djibouti, form a temporary government.

2001   Islamist terrorists attack targets in the United States. The United States suspects that terrorists are hiding out in Somalia.

2004   Somali politicians form the Transitional Federal Government. Abdullahi Yusuf Ahmed becomes president of Somalia.

2006   The Islamic Courts Union (ICU) militia takes over Mogadishu and other parts of Somalia. Government troops fight ICU forces for control of the nation.

COUNTRY NAME Somali Democratic Republic

AREA 246,201 square miles (637,657 square km)

MAIN LANDFORMS Benadir Coast, Guban Plain, Haud Plain, Kar Kar Mountains, Mudug Plain, Nugaaleed Valley, Ogo Plateau

HIGHEST POINT Surud Ad, 7,900 feet (2,408 meters)

LOWEST POINT sea level

MAJOR RIVERS Shabeelle, Jubba

ANIMALS antelopes, cheetahs, gazelles, hornbills, hyenas, larks, leopards, lizards, naked mole rats, pigeons, snakes, termites

CAPITAL CITY Mogadishu

OTHER MAJOR CITIES Berbera, Hargeysa, Kismaayo

OFFICIAL LANGUAGE Somali

MONETARY UNIT Somali shilling. 1 shilling = 100 cents

SOMALI CURRENCY

The unit of currency in Somalia is the Somali shilling. One shilling is divided into one hundred cents. The Central Bank of Somalia issued coins and paper money until 1990. It issued 5-, 10-, 20-, 100-, 500-, and 1,000-shilling notes (paper money), 1-, 5-, 10-, and 50-cent coins, and a 1-shilling coin. After warfare engulfed the country, no new currency was printed. (Somaliland introduced its own shilling in 1995.)

Somali shillings have become old and ragged, but they are still in use. People also buy and sell with U.S. dollars. Sometimes people barter, or exchange goods and services, instead of exchanging money. In 2006 it took 1,340 Somali shillings to equal one U.S. dollar.

The national flag of Somalia is pale blue, with a large five-pointed white star in the center. This flag was first used in 1954, when Italy controlled Somalia. It was adopted in 1960 as the flag of a newly independent Somalia.

The star represents freedom, and the five points stand for five historical branches of the Somali people: those in Italian Somaliland, British Somaliland, French Somaliland (Djibouti), the Ogaden region of Ethiopia, and northeastern Kenya.

Independent Somaliland has had its own flag since 1997. This flag has three horizontal stripes in green, white, and red. Across the top green stripe, white writing in the Arabic language expresses faith in Allah. A black star rests in the middle of the white stripe.

Somalia created its first national anthem in 1960, when it became independent. In 2000 the transitional government adopted a new national anthem, in hopes that it would inspire Somalis to heal their country's wounds. The anthem is a well-known folksong by an unknown composer. The title, "Somaliyaay Toosoo," means "Somalia Wake Up." The anthem consists of six verses and a chorus. Here is the chorus in English:

Somalia wake up,
Wake up and join hands together
And we must help the weakest of our people
All the time.

For a link to a website where you can listen to the Somali national anthem, "Somaliyaay Toosoo" (Somalia Wake Up), visit www.vgsbooks.com.

ABDI ABDIRAHMAN (b. 1977) Born in Mogadishu, this athlete moved to Arizona with his family when he was thirteen. He took up running five years later, when he began studies at a local community college. He showed such promise that he transferred to the University of Arizona to train. A distance runner, he is a two-time U.S. 10,000-meter champion and a two-time U.S. 10-mile (16-km) champion.

IMAN ABDULMAJID (b. 1955) This former model and businesswoman, known mainly by her first name, Iman, is the daughter of a Somali diplomat. She was born in Mogadishu. While she was studying at Nairobi University in 1975, a professional photographer noticed her good looks. She did her first modeling job for *Vogue* magazine and quickly became a supermodel. She went on to create a line of cosmetics for women of color. She has also written books and acted in films. She is married to singer David Bowie.

ABDULLAHI YUSUF AHMED (b. 1934) Born in central Somalia, this politician studied in Italy and the former Soviet Union. He became a Somali army commander in the 1960s. After taking part in an unsuccessful plot to overthrow President Siad Barre in 1978, he escaped to Kenya. From there he led a rebel movement against the dictator. He was jailed in Ethiopia and released in 1991. Following his return to Somalia, he became a warlord and president of Puntland. In 2004 he became president of Somalia's Transitional Federal Government.

NURUDDIN FARAH (b. 1945) This award-winning author was born in Baydhabo in southern Somalia. He attended university in India and studied theater in London. His first novel, published in English in 1970, was titled *From a Crooked Rib.* The work won praise from feminist groups because it examined the theme of women's rights. Farah has also written about the violence of his homeland and the relationship between rich and poor countries. Farah speaks five languages—English, Somali, Arabic, Italian, and French. He has lived most of his adult life in Europe and the United States.

ALI MOHAMED GHEDI (b. 1952) Trained as a veterinarian in Somalia and Italy, Ghedi worked as a researcher and lecturer at the National University of Somalia until the outbreak of the civil war. He then became a consultant to the livestock industry. He also served as president of an association of nongovernmental organizations. In this job, he worked to bring peace to war-torn Somalia. He became prime minister of the Transitional Federal Government in 2004. Ghedi was born in Mogadishu.

MAHAMMAD ABDILLE HASAN (1864–1920) The man known to the British as the Mad Mullah was born at a small watering place in British Somaliland. He began studying the Quran at age seven. During a pilgrimage to Mecca in 1894, he joined a Sufi brotherhood. Returning to British Somaliland, he urged people to strictly observe the Muslim faith and to expel the British. Through his speeches and poetry, he attracted many followers. He led a twenty-year resistance against the British and the Ethiopians.

DAHIR RIYALE KAHIN (b. 1952) Born in British Somaliland, this politician studied in the former Soviet Union. Returning to Somalia, he became a diplomat, district governor, and businessperson. He served as vice president of Somaliland from 1997 to 2002 and took over as president when the president died. He then won election as president of Somaliland in 2003.

HALIMA KHALIIF OMAR (1948–2004) This well-known singer, nicknamed Magool (meaning "flower"), began her career when she was a child in Mogadishu. In the 1970s, when Somalia was at war with Ethiopia, she sang patriotic songs. Later, she moved to London, England. When she returned for a concert in the Mogadishu stadium in 1987, an estimated fifteen thousand people attended. She died in Amsterdam, Holland.

K'NAAN WARSAME (b. 1978) This rap artist was born in Mogadishu. When he was thirteen, his family moved to the United States and then to Toronto, Canada. He has performed in internationally televised concerts and toured extensively. He performs in English but sings about Somali issues.

Sights to See

Travel Warning: The U.S. Department of State warns U.S. citizens against all travel to Somalia, including Somaliland. Interclan and interfactional fighting can flare up with little warning, and kidnapping, murder, and other threats to U.S. citizens and other foreigners can occur unpredictably in many regions. Visit www.travel.state.gov for updates on the safety of travel.

BERBERA AIRSTRIP More than 2.5 miles (4 km) in length, this is one of the world's longest airstrips (a runway without an airport). Engineers from the former Soviet Union helped build the airstrip. NASA, the U.S. space agency, once rented it as an emergency landing strip for the space shuttle.

FAKHR AL-DIN MOSQUE Built in 1269 out of coral blocks, this mosque is the oldest known building in Mogadishu and one of the oldest buildings on the coast of East Africa. The rectangular building has lobbies, courtyards, and a spacious prayer hall with a high domed ceiling. It was built for the first sultan of Mogadishu.

LAAS GA'AL CAVE PAINTINGS In 2003 a French archaeologist discovered these prehistoric paintings inside a cave near Hargeysa. The paintings showed a cow and what looked like a person praying to the cow. Other nearby paintings depicted donkeys and goats. The cave may have been used as a temple.

MOGADISHU Although visiting is not safe, Mogadishu is home to numerous pre–civil war landmarks, including the Arba Rucun Mosque with its needle-nosed tower; the sultan of Oman's fort, known as the Garessa; an Italian-built cathedral; modern hotels; government buildings; and busy marketplaces. Almost every city building has been damaged or destroyed, however.

SHRINE OF YUSUF AW BARKHADLE Yusuf Aw Barkhadle was a Muslim religious teacher who came to Somalia from Arabia. He probably arrived in the 1100s. Located west of Hargeysa, his tomb is sacred to Muslims. In fact, making three pilgrimages to the tomb is considered the equivalent of a trip to Mecca. Aw Barkhadle introduced Arabian black-headed sheep to Somalia.

civil war: a war between opposing groups of citizens in the same country

clan: a large network of families whose members trace their history to a common ancestor

corruption: widespread dishonesty, bribery, and other illegal activity within a government or other organization

drought: a long period without rain, during which crops wither or won't grow

irrigation: a system of pipes, pumps, ponds, and other devices, used for carrying water to crops

Islam: A religion founded on the Arabian Peninsula in the A.D. 600s. People who practice the Islamic religion are called Muslims.

Islamists: Muslims who want to establish Islamic societies governed by Islamic law

nationalism: a philosophy that emphasizes loyalty to one's own nation above all else. Nationalist goals may include preservation of national culture, fulfillment of the nation's needs, and the nation's independence from outside influence.

nomad: a person who travels from place to place to make a living. Most nomads travel to find water and grazing land for their animals.

pilgrimage: a journey to a holy place

refugee: a person who flees, usually to a foreign country, to escape danger in his or her homeland

remittance: a sum of money sent to another person. Immigrants sometimes send remittances to family members in their homeland.

riverine: living or situated on the banks of a river

sharia law: law based on the teachings of the Quran, the Islamic holy book, and the hadith, or sayings and deeds of the prophet Muhammad

socialism: a political and economic system in which the government controls large sectors of the economy, with limited private property or private business ownership

warlord: a military commander, independent of an official state army, who uses force to rule a territory

Glossary

Abdullahi, Mohamed Diriye. *Culture and Customs of Somalia.* **Westport, CT: Greenwood Press, 2001.**
Part of a series on the culture and customs of Africa, this book begins with an overview of Somali history and continues with chapters on religion, the arts, food, and social customs.

Besteman, Catherine. *Unraveling Somalia: Race, Violence, and the Legacy of Slavery.* **Philadelphia: University of Pennsylvania Press, 1999.**
This book disagrees with the prevalent view that the conflict in Somali society stems from clan rivalries. The author suggests that much of the violence is related to racial and class differences, regional identities, and a struggle to control valuable land.

Central Intelligence Agency (CIA). "Somalia." *The World Factbook,* **2006.**
http://www.cia.gov/cia/publications/factbook/geos/so.html (April 2006).
This online document provides a brief outline of Somalia's geography, population, government, and economy.

Europa World Year Book 2005. **Vol. 2. 46th ed. New York: Routledge, 2005.**
The article on Somalia in this reference book details political events since 1991.

"Internally Displaced Somalis Face Uncertain Future after Years of State Collapse." *Relief Web,* **2004.**
http://wwwnotes.reliefweb.int/w/rwb.nsf/vID/
C1499D046B7C08E8C1256F560052735B?OpenDocument (April 2006).
This paper examines the causes and effects of internal displacement in Somalia.

Kusow, Abdi M., ed. *Putting the Cart Before the Horse: Contested Nationalism and the Crisis of the Nation-State in Somalia.* **Trenton, NJ: Red Sea Press, 2004.**
This collection of essays by scholars examines various aspects of Somali nationalism and history.

Lewis, I. M. *Understanding Somalia: Guide to Culture, History and Social Institutions.* **2nd ed. London: Haan Associates, 1993.**
This book, by a British anthropologist who has made the study of the Somali people his life's work, offers a brief overview of Somali culture and history.

Little, Peter D. *Somalia: Economy without State.* **Bloomington: Indiana University Press, 2003.**
The author, a U.S. anthropologist, examines how clan elders, religious leaders, and businesspeople have worked together to bring some order to life in Somalia. He looks at how economic life continues, despite the absence of a government.

Menkhaus, Ken. "Somalia: Situation and Trend Analysis."
Schweizerische Flüüchtlingshilfe, 2004.
http://www.ecoi.net/pub/ts33_040920_SOM_update_e.pdf (April 2006).
Menkhaus is a consultant on Somali issues to the United Nations and the
U.S. government. In this paper, he examines recent political trends in
Somalia and Somaliland.

**Mohamed, Abdullahi Elmi. "Somalia's Degrading Environment:
Causes and Effects of Deforestation and Hazardous Waste Dumping
in Somalia."** *Somali Centre for Water and the Environment*, 2001.
http://www.banadir.com/a.htm (April 2006).
This paper looks at some of the environmental issues facing Somalia.

**Putman, Diana Briton, and Mohammod Cabdi Noor. "The Somalis:
Their History and Culture."** *Center for Applied Linguistics*, 1993.
(April 2006).
http://www.culturalorientation.net/somali/somtxt.html
This fact sheet, written to help people who work with Somali refugees in the
United States, includes the meanings of many Somali names and expressions.

"Socio-Economic Survey 2002: Somalia." *UNDP Somalia and World
Bank*, 2003.
http://siteresources.worldbank.org/INTSOMALIA/Resources/swb_complete_report
.pdf (April 2006).
The United Nations Development Program and the World Bank conducted a
nationwide survey of Somali households in 2002. The survey collected data on
people's age, income, housing, and access to services. This site provides the
survey results.

"Somalia." *Population Reference Bureau*, 2005.
http://www.prb.org (click on "Data by Country," and then "Somalia") (April 2006).
This site offers country-by-country statistics on health, family planning,
poverty, and other topics.

"Somali Acacia-Commiphora Bushlands and Thickets." *World
Wildlife Fund*, 2001.
http://www.worldwildlife.org/wildworld/profiles/terrestrial/at/at0715_full.html
(April 2006).
This article describes the ecological zone that dominates Somalia.

"Somalia: A Country Study." *Library of Congress, Federal Research
Division*, 1992.
http://memory.loc.gov/frd/cs/sotoc.html (April 2006).
This online document covers the history, society, and economy of this troubled country.

**UN Office for the Coordination of Humanitarian Affairs. "Latest
News from Somalia."** *IRINnews.org*, 2006.
http://www.irinnews.org/frontpage.asp?SelectRegion=Horn_of
_Africa&SelectCountry=Somalia (April 2006).
This website covers developments in Somalia, including a chronology of the
year's events, feature stories, and interviews.

Andrzejewski, B. W., and I. M. Lewis. *Somali Poetry: An Introduction.* Oxford: Oxford University Press, 1964.
This book provides an introduction to Somali culture, language, poetry, and poets. It includes examples of classical poems and traditional and modern songs in Somali and English, as well as translations of religious poetry from Arabic.

"Arts Midwest." *Midwest World Fest,* 2005.
http://midwestworldfest.org/student/somalia/
This page has many interesting links to sites related to Somali culture, geography, and history.

Barnes, Virginia Lee, and Janice Boddy. *Aman: The Story of a Somali Girl.* Toronto: Knopf, 1994.
This book tells the true story of a teenage Somali girl, Aman, forced to marry an older man she hates.

Bowden, Mark. "Black Hawk Down." *The Inquirer,* November 16, 1997.
http://inquirer.philly.com/packages/somalia/nov16/rang16.asp
Mark Bowden, a staff writer with the *Philadelphia Inquirer* newspaper, tells what happened on October 3, 1993, when a quick raid on a Mogadishu house by an elite squad of U.S. troops turned into a disaster. A movie was later made about this raid.

Burton, Sir Richard. *First Footsteps in East Africa.* Edited with an introduction and additional chapters by Gordon Waterfield. London: Routledge and Kegan Paul, 1966.
In this fascinating account of his expedition to Harer in 1854, Sir Richard Burton described the plants and animals he came across and the character and habits of the Somali people he encountered.

"Country Profile: Somalia." *BBC News.*
http://news.bbc.co.uk/2/hi/africa/country_profiles/1072592.stm
This basic overview includes links to feature articles about Somali political leaders, daily life in a lawless society, and political developments.

Dirie, Waris, and Cathleen Miller. *Desert Flower.* New York: William Morrow and Company, 1998.
This is the autobiography of a famous fashion model who grew up in a traditional nomadic Somali family. At age five, she underwent female genital mutilation. At thirteen she ran away to avoid being married to an old man. She was almost raped several times. Despite the frightening and horrifying things she endured, her story is inspirational.

Farah, Nuruddin. *Links.* New York: Penguin Books, 2005.
This novel tells what happens to a Somali-born American when he returns to war-ravaged Mogadishu to visit his mother's grave. He discovers that nothing is what it seems to be.

Nabwire, Constance, and Bertha Vining Montgomery. *Cooking the East African Way.* Minneapolis: Lerner Publications Company, 2002.
This cookbook contains recipes from Somalia and other East African countries. Various cultural information is also included.

Further Reading and Websites

Laurence, Margaret. *The Prophet's Camel Bell.* **Toronto: McLelland and Stewart, 1963.**
The writer (who later became one of Canada's best-known novelists) spent two years in the early 1950s with her engineer husband getting to known camel herders in the Haud region of Somaliland. This book is alternatively titled *New Wind in a Dry Land.*

Mogadishu: Images from the Past
http://www.swan.ac.uk/cds/rd/mogimage.htm
The website has links to historic drawings, maps, photographs, and descriptions of a beautiful city that lies in ruins.

"MSF Focus on Somalia: Caught in the Storm." *Medecins Sans Frontieres.*
http://www.msf.org/msfinternational/invoke.cfm?objectid=DCE47CA2-E018-0C72
-09DA1799321C94C7&component=toolkit.article&method=full_html
This series of five articles describes conditions in Somalia, as seen by volunteer health workers with the medical aid agency Medecins Sans Frontieres (Doctors Without Borders).

"Places That Don't Exist," *Shoot and Scribble.com.*
http://dspace.dial.pipex.com/town/estate/de44/sr/page6/page15/page15.html
British journalist Simon Reeve traveled to Somaliland to make a television documentary. Some of his photographs are posted on this website.

Republic of Somaliland: Country Profile
http://www.somalilandgov.com/
The official homepage of Somaliland has a profile of the country's people, geography, and resources, and news releases about events.

"Somalia." *Relief Web.*
http://www.reliefweb.int/rw/dbc.nsf/doc104?OpenForm&rc=1&cc=som
This website compiles emergency alerts about drought, famine, flood, and violence in Somalia.

vgsbooks.com
http://www.vgsbooks.com
Visit vgsbooks.com, the homepage of the Visual Geography Series®. You can get linked to all sorts of useful on-line information, including geographical, historical, demographic, cultural, and economic websites. The vgsbooks.com site is a great resource for late-breaking news and statistics.

language, 44, 48, 50, 51, 63, 68
livestock, 4, 14, 15, 34, 58, 59, 60, 64

manufacturing, 57, 58
maps, 6, 11
media and communications, 50, 51, 52, 63
militias, 7, 34, 42, 45, 60, 65; Islamic Courts Union, 7, 36–37, 50, 64, 67; landmines, 41; in Mogadishu, 18, 32, 33
Mogadishu, 12, 15, 17–18, 30, 36, 42, 44, 50; Bakara market, 61; as capital, 7, 17, 29, 35, 64, 65, 67, 68, 72; clothing, 53; early history, 21, 22, 23, 25, 66; Hawiye clan, 32; industry, 59; media, 63; Mogadishu University, 46; mosque, 48–49, 72; music, 51; Somali Youth League (SYL), 28, 29, 30, 66; transportation, 62; warlords in, 18, 33, 50
mountains, 4, 12, 14, 60; Kar Kar Mountains, 8–9, 68; Surud Ad, 9, 68
music, 50, 51–52, 63

natural resources, 14–15
nomads, 46, 49, 51, 53, 54, 55, 63, 67. *See also* herders

Omar, Halima Khaliif, 71

pirates, 36
poetry, 50–51, 55
population, 38, 39, 65
Population Reference Bureau, 38, 39
ports, 7, 10, 17, 18, 19, 33, 36, 62. *See also* Berbera
poverty, 7, 15, 56
Puntland, 7, 19, 34, 41, 44, 45, 67

al-Qaeda, 34, 61

refugee camps, 38–39, 47; IDP camps, 42, 43; Qoryoley Refugee Camp, 4–5
regions: Benadir Coast, 9–10, 25, 68; Guban Plain, 8, 68; Kar Kar Mountains, 8–9, 68; Mudug Plain, 9, 68; Nugaaleed Valley, 9, 68; Ogo

Plateau, 9, 68
remittances, 43, 58, 60–61, 64
Republic of Somaliland, 7, 18, 19, 21, 38, 65; currency, 68; economy, 64; education, 46; establishment of, 33, 35, 67; ethnic groups, 44; flag, 69; holidays and festivals, 55; landmines, 41; transportation, 62, 63. *See also* Berbera; Hargeysa
rivers, 9, 12; Jubba, 4, 5, 9, 10, 14, 18, 63, 68; Shabeelle, 4, 5, 9, 10, 14, 68

Siad Barre, Mohamed, 7, 30–33, 44, 63, 64, 67, 70
Somalia: boundaries, location, and size, 4, 8; currency, 34, 60, 61, 68; emigrants and refugees from, 7, 31, 32, 34, 38, 43, 56, 59, 64, 65; flag, 31, 69; flora and fauna, 8, 12, 13–14, 16, 17, 60, 68; government, 4, 7, 17, 33–36, 60; maps, 6, 11; national anthem, 69; official name, 8, 67, 68
Somali National Movement (SNM), 32, 33, 67
sports and games, 54–55

topography, 4, 8–10
trade, 60–61
transportation, 33, 34, 56, 59, 62–63, 65

United Nations, 7, 28, 33, 38, 43, 45, 66, 67; feeding center, 40
United States, 36, 43; aid to Somalia, 30, 32; Operation Restore Hope, 7, 33, 67; September 11, 2001, attacks, 34, 61, 67

warlords, 7, 36, 37, 64, 65; Adid, Mohammed, 32; control of country, 16, 56, 57; landmines, 41; in Mogadishu, 18, 33, 50; in poetry, 51
women, 16, 38–39, 40, 43, 46–47, 50, 52, 53; female genital mutilation (FGM), 40
World Health Organization, 38, 41
World War I, 27
World War II, 28, 66

Captions for photos appearing on cover and chapter openers:

Cover: Somalis make their homes at a refugee camp on the Somali-Kenya border after fleeing the civil war in the 1990s.

pp. 4–5 Many Somalis live at the Qoryoley Refugee Camp in southern Somalia.

pp. 8–9 The town of Baraawe sits on the coast south of Mogadishu.

pp. 38–39 A group of Somali women in traditional tribal dress pose for a picture in the early 1990s. A group of Somali men stands behind them.

pp. 48–49 A mosque in Mogadishu

pp. 56–57 Somali men and women sell fresh fruits and vegetables along a street lined with shops in Mogadishu.

Photo Acknowledgments
The images in this book are used with the permission of: © Jason Laure, pp. 4–5, 8–9, 52, 56–57; © XNR Productions, pp. 6, 11; © Clive Shirley/Panos Pictures, p. 10; © Steve Kaufman/CORBIS, p. 13; © C. Hayslip/Travel-Images.com, pp. 14, 48–49, 58; © Getty Images, pp. 16, 23, 24, 26, 35, 37, 40, 41, 42; © Scheufler Collection/CORBIS, p. 18–19; © Mohamed Ibrahim Isak/Panapress/Getty Images, p. 19; © Bettmann/CORBIS, p. 29; © KPA/ZUMA Press, p. 30; © Norbert Schiller/The Image Works, p. 32; © Peter Turnley/CORBIS, p. 38–39; © Liba Taylor/CORBIS, p. 45; © Kevin Fleming/CORBIS, pp. 46, 54; © Sven Torfinn/Panos Pictures, p. 61; © Yann Arthus-Bertrand/CORBIS, p. 62; Audrius Tomonis—www.banknotes.com, p. 68; © Laura Westlund/Independent Picture Service, p. 69.

Front cover: © Christophe Calais/In Visu/CORBIS.

Back cover: NASA.